The Future of Transatlantic Relations

*Report of an Independent Task Force
Sponsored by the
Council on Foreign Relations*

Robert D. Blackwill,
Chairman and Project Director

The Council on Foreign Relations, Inc., a nonprofit, nonpartisan national membership organization founded in 1921, is dedicated to promoting understanding of international affairs through the free and civil exchange of ideas. The Council's members are dedicated to the belief that America's peace and prosperity are firmly linked to that of the world. From this flows the mission of the Council: to foster America's understanding of its fellow members of the international community, near and far, their peoples, cultures, histories, hopes, quarrels, and ambitions, and thus to serve, protect, and advance America's own global interests through study and debate, private and public.

THE COUNCIL TAKES NO INSTITUTIONAL POSITION ON POLICY ISSUES AND HAS NO AFFILIATION WITH THE U.S. GOVERNMENT. ALL STATEMENTS OF FACT AND EXPRESSIONS OF OPINION CONTAINED IN ALL ITS PUBLICATIONS ARE THE SOLE RESPONSIBILITY OF THE AUTHOR OR AUTHORS.

The Council will sponsor an Independent Task Force when (1) an issue of current and critical importance to U.S. foreign policy arises, and (2) it seems that a group diverse in backgrounds and perspectives may, nonetheless, be able to reach a meaningful consensus on a policy through private and nonpartisan deliberations. Typically, a Task Force meets between two and five times over a brief period to ensure the relevance of its work.

Upon reaching a conclusion, a Task Force issues a Report, and the Council publishes its text and posts it on the Council web site. Task Force Reports can take three forms: (1) a strong and meaningful policy consensus, with Task Force members endorsing the general policy thrust and judgments reached by the group, though not necessarily every finding and recommendation; (2) a Report stating the various policy positions, each as sharply and fairly as possible; or (3) a "Chairman's Report," where Task Force members who agree with the Chairman's Report may associate themselves with it, while those who disagree may submit dissenting statements. Upon reaching a conclusion, Task Forces may also ask individuals who were not members of the Task Force to associate themselves with the Task Force Report to enhance its impact. All Task Force Reports "benchmark" their findings against current administration policy in order to make explicit areas of agreement and disagreement. The Task Force is solely responsible for its Report. The Council takes no institutional position.

For further information about the Council or this Task Force, please write the Council on Foreign Relations, 58 East 68th Street, New York, NY 10021, or call the Director of Communications at (212) 434-9400. Visit our web site at www.foreignrelations.org.

CONTENTS

FOREWORD

Throughout the Cold War, the United States and Western Europe were inextricably bound together in the Atlantic alliance by the requirement to deter Soviet aggression in Europe. The overwhelming danger posed by Moscow served to cement this alliance, suppressing or at least minimizing differences, and making common defense the defining characteristic of transatlantic relations. As the Soviet empire and system crumbled, many policymakers and scholars at the time worried that the absence of this threat would significantly weaken alliance cohesion and ultimately damage the broader U.S.-European relationship.

With these concerns in mind, the Council on Foreign Relations sponsored this Independent Task Force on the Future of Transatlantic Relations. We chose Robert D. Blackwill, a widely respected former career diplomat and Harvard scholar, to serve as Chairman and Project Director and to author the Task Force Report. We also invited a highly diverse and experienced corps of American and European policymakers, diplomats, analysts, and business and opinion leaders to participate in the Task Force deliberations. The Council wishes to thank all of them for their time and contributions.

Strikingly, despite differences on specific points or tactical issues, Task Force members agreed clearly and strongly on the inherent value of the transatlantic relationship and the merit of endeavoring to create a more vigorous and robust partnership capable of addressing a diverse set of international concerns over the long term. Intrinsic in every prescription is the conviction that protecting U.S. and European interests in the period ahead would certainly benefit from intensified transatlantic cooperation. While some might argue that there are other conceivable global partners for the United States, the report effectively argues that the U.S.-European relationship must be at the center of American efforts to forge a new world order. As the Council forwards this report, we hope that it will contribute to the current policy debate on both sides of the Atlantic and help stimulate a more comprehensive assessment in Washington, Brussels, and other European capitals on the opportunities that currently exist for the transatlantic partners to shape the international system in the next decade and beyond.

Leslie H. Gelb
President,
Council on Foreign Relations

ACKNOWLEDGMENTS

Over the past year, the Independent Task Force on the Future of Transatlantic Relations, sponsored by the Council on Foreign Relations, and this report, have benefited from the assistance of many people. I am especially indebted to the members of the Task Force and observers from both the Clinton administration and European diplomatic missions in Washington, and to the many presenters who admirably helped guide our discussions. Without the hard work, dedication, and wise counsel of all of these colleagues, this project would not have been successful.

I am delighted that all 40 members of the Task Force endorse the broad thrust of this report, although not all have signed on to every word or prescription in this volume, and some have registered additional views or specific dissents. The willingness of all Task Force participants—members and observers—to share their time, thoughts, and expertise has significantly enriched this report. In particular, I wish to thank Ambassador Jürgen Chrobog of the Federal Republic of Germany, Ambassador Hugo Paemen of the Delegation of the European Commission to the United States, Ambassador Ferdinando Salleo of Italy, and Ambassador K. Erik Tygesen of Denmark for their regular participation and always insightful advice.

My gratitude also goes to the European Commission of the European Union for its generous financial support of this project. In this respect, I appreciate the assistance provided by John Richardson and Jonathan Davidson of the commission's Washington Delegation.

At the Council on Foreign Relations, I would like to acknowledge Council President Leslie H. Gelb, who was instrumental in the creation of this Task Force, and Paula Dobriansky, Vice President and Director of the Council's Washington Program, and her staff for arranging our numerous meetings. Edward Fogarty, a research associate at the Council, also provided enthusiastic support to the Task Force at every stage and helped ensure that this effort remained on course.

Finally, I am grateful to my staff at the John F. Kennedy School of Government. My warm thanks go to Leigh Morris, for her research and logistical assistance, as well as to Amy Clemons and Jennifer McLeod, for their administrative support and help in the final production stages. I owe a special debt to Kristin Archick, who coauthored with me a set of analytical background papers for the Task Force (which may be found on the Council's web site at http://www.foreignrelations.org), and whose assistance was invaluable in countless ways throughout the life of this project.

Robert D. Blackwill
Chairman and Project Director

EXECUTIVE SUMMARY

This report addresses the current state and the future prospects for the transatlantic relationship. The broad challenge the U.S.-European partnership faces in the period ahead is threefold: to persuade others around the world in post–Cold War conditions to abide by internationally accepted norms and patterns of behavior and the rules of the international institutions that embody them; to deal skillfully with the emerging new power centers, of which China and India are the most prominent; and to meet the current serious threats to Western interests, especially in the Middle East, when these threats often seem to ordinary citizens more remote, abstract, and complex than during the Cold War. This daunting effort will clearly require transatlantic policies that involve a delicate and flexible combination of incentives and disincentives applied to these other countries in a highly discriminating manner in widely differing circumstances. Designing and sustaining such policies will be no easy task for Western governments with compelling domestic preoccupations in the full glare of the media spotlight.

Transatlantic relations are on an even keel. Although Suez demonstrated in 1956 that sudden policy differences could fundamentally disrupt the alliance almost overnight, and while the Asian and global economic crises and the chaos in Russia continue to worry the United States and Europe deeply, there are currently no serious disputes across the Atlantic and none on the horizon. Indeed, the transatlantic partnership can be proud that in recent years it has ejected Iraq from Kuwait; stopped the killing in Bosnia; projected stability and democracy eastward through the enlargement of NATO to Poland, the Czech Republic, and Hungary; intensified a parallel stabilizing enlargement process within the European Union (EU); made extraordinary progress in Northern Ireland; managed security relations with Russia, at least this far, without a serious blowup; and—despite the current global economic dislocations—together produced a new burst of transatlantic mergers, acquisitions, and investments and led the struggle to open up further the international trading system.

With U.S. vital interests connected to Europe relatively safe for the foreseeable future, Washington's security preoccupations are turning more and more toward those regions where vital American interests are threatened—most particularly in the greater Middle East and, to a lesser and more potential degree, in the Asia-Pacific region. In these crucial areas, the state of transatlantic cooperation is far less bright than on the continent. In the greater Middle East, the two sides of the Atlantic differ on the tactics for dealing with virtually every issue in the region: the Israel-Palestinian peace process; Western interaction with Iran; how best to slow proliferation of weapons of mass destruction into the area; the role of force in defending transatlantic interests in the region; and increasingly, even how best to deal with Saddam Hussein over the longer term. As for Western security challenges in Asia, including managing the rise of Chinese power, instability on the Korean peninsula, and the growing importance of India, the Europeans are virtually absent in any strategic sense. These issues regarding transatlantic collaboration outside of Europe could again raise traditional burden-sharing problems across the Atlantic.

The United States and Europe are the only conceivable global partners for each other in seeking to shape the international system in positive ways into the next century. Without America, Europe will tend to retreat into a continental fortress mentality or into sustained passivity as threats from beyond the continent progressively build and then intrude into the interests and daily lives of the allies. Without Europe, the United States will likely alternate between brief and usually ineffective spasms of unilateralism interspersed with occasional temptations to withdraw substantially from messy international life. A growing transatlantic partnership consistent with the regional and global challenges of the next century will increasingly protect the vital and important interests of both the United States and Europe, and thus the basic welfare of their citizens. As Henry Kissinger has put it, "On both sides of the

Atlantic, the next phase of our foreign policy will require restoration of some of the dedication, attitudes and convictions of common destiny that brought us to this point—though, of course, under totally new conditions." This will entail deliberate and sustained statesmanship as well as innumerable acts of detailed and coordinated policy implementation on the part of Europe and the United States over many years. There is no time to waste.

PRESCRIPTIONS

A crucial point to emphasize at the outset of this report is that notable opportunities presently exist for the U.S.-European relationship to help mold the international environment of the coming period. The two sides of the Atlantic continue to share enduring vital interests and face a common set of challenges both in Europe and beyond. These challenges are so many and diverse that neither the United States nor the allies can adequately address these regional and global concerns alone, especially in light of growing domestic constraints on the implementation of foreign policy. Thus, promoting shared interests and managing common threats to the West in the years ahead will necessitate not only continued cooperation but an intensified transatlantic partnership.

However, this main theme of the report—that the United States should draw Europe over time much further into a global strategic partnership to help shape the international system in the new era—does not appear to be a sustained and effective priority of the Clinton administration. To create such a partnership would require more vigorous and active presidential and congressional leadership than has often been seen in recent years. Although this report contains over 40 policy recommendations on various political, security, and economic aspects of the transatlantic relationship, the following prescriptions are critical. They seek to strengthen the collaboration between the two sides of the Atlantic on issues central to promoting a secure and stable Europe and to build on these achievements to enable the United States and the allies to tackle cooperatively the myriad challenges likely to confront the international system in the period ahead. Thus, they represent the heart of a revitalized effort to be carried out every day by governments on both sides of the Atlantic to create a global U.S.-European partnership:

- The EU and allied governments should play a more active private and more visible public part in attempting to manage with the United States the regional and global implications of the Asian economic crises. This includes a comprehensive reform of international financial architecture.

- The greatest threat to vital transatlantic interests in Europe is the weak internal security surrounding Russia's nuclear weapons and material as well as its chemical and biological arsenal. While the United States is not doing enough to address this danger, the allies are doing almost nothing. This should urgently change; the Europeans should spend much more money on the problem.

- Despite the current enormous difficulties inside Russia, the West should continue to do what it responsibly can to promote economic reform within the country, if the Russian government takes the necessary steps, and increase greatly its support for democratic institution building in Russia.

- NATO should put an end to all military conflict in the Balkans and keep it that way.

- After the entry of Poland, the Czech Republic, and Hungary into NATO in 1999, there should be an informal pause for at least three to five years before any new candidates are invited to join the alliance.

- The United States and the European Union should begin to negotiate step by step a genuinely open trade and investment area—a true single transatlantic market—with real deadlines.

- Both the United States and Europe should work harder to help ensure Turkey's Western orientation.

- NATO should conceptually broaden its new Strategic Concept to deal with threats to shared Western interests beyond Europe, especially in the Middle East: to protect Gulf oil, to slow the entry of weapons of mass destruction and missile delivery systems into that region, and to undertake the long-term joint military planning necessary to prepare for these contingencies.

- Western Europe should substantially accelerate its military modernization and power projection capability in order to have the option of joining the United States effectively in defending Western vital interests in the greater Middle East with force, if that should become necessary. This includes intensified U.S.-European work on theater ballistic missile defenses, stand-off forces, and defense industry cooperation across the Atlantic.

- The United States should maintain the clear lead in mediating negotiations between Israel and its neighbors. The EU's role should nevertheless grow over time. Europeans have a right to expect that Washington confront directly and strongly either one, or both, of the parties when their policies are thwarting the peace process.

- The United States and Europe should accelerate efforts to reinvigorate the Gulf War coalition and resume the use of sustained force against Iraq if Saddam Hussein continues to take provocative action. At the same time, the U.N. Security Council should maintain the economic sanctions on Baghdad into the foreseeable future and rigorously enforce those sanctions so as to try to deny Iraq materials that could be utilized for its WMD and ballistic missile programs.

- With respect to Iran, the United States and Europe need to forge a new strategy and opening toward Iran based on a specific set of agreed criteria regarding Tehran's external behavior. The allies should become much more engaged in the effort to slow Iran's acquisition of weapons of mass destruction.

- The EU and individual European governments that are now animated regarding Asia almost entirely by commercial objectives should increasingly bring the region—in particular the rise of Chinese power, Japan, the Korean peninsula, and India—into their strategic calculations and international security perspectives. This will require a concerted American effort to involve the allies much more in developing analyses and policy options regarding Asia.

• Cooperative efforts to combat international terrorism, environmental degradation, organized crime, and narcotics trafficking should be strengthened within the transatlantic community.

I. INTRODUCTION

This report addresses the current state and the future prospects for the transatlantic relationship. A crucial point to emphasize at the outset of this report is that notable opportunities presently exist for the U.S.-European relationship to help mold the next century's world. The two sides of the Atlantic continue to share enduring vital interests and face a common set of challenges both in Europe and beyond. These challenges are so many and diverse that neither the United States nor the allies can adequately address these regional and global concerns alone, especially in light of growing domestic constraints on the implementation of foreign policy. Thus, protecting shared interests and managing common threats to the West in the years ahead will necessitate not only continued cooperation but a broader and more comprehensive transatlantic partnership than in the past.

The prescriptions contained in this report seek to intensify such a partnership. Some reinforce current administration policy, especially with respect to European security and political economy. Some policy suggestions go against administration policies, particularly outside Europe. The entire thrust of these ambitious prescriptions, however, requires more vigorous and active presidential and congressional leadership than has often been seen in recent years. The most important departure from present U.S. policy is the report's emphasis on drawing Europe concretely over time much further into a global strategic partnership with the United States to help shape the international system in the new era.

Harmony across the Atlantic is not a goal in itself, but rather an instrument to improve the security and well-being of societies on both sides of the Atlantic and of the world. Other nations have begun to play important regional roles, but only U.S.-European collaboration has a proven track record for positive global leadership over a sustained period. Moreover, this transatlantic leadership is particularly crucial in an era characterized, as the Asian and global economic crises have vividly demonstrated, by increasing international interdependence. This latter trend has also shown the growing importance of matters of political economy in the international system at the expense of the quite reasonable commanding Cold War emphasis on military security necessitated by the reality of Soviet military power. As the mid-December 1998 attack on Iraq by the United States and Britain demonstrates, the threatened and actual use of force still has a legitimate place in transatlantic policies, but that role is substantially smaller and more complicated to implement than in the past.

The current broad challenge that the U.S.-European partnership faces in the period ahead is to persuade others around the world in post–Cold War conditions to abide by internationally accepted norms and patterns of behavior, and the rules of the international institutions that embody them; to deal skillfully with the emerging new power centers, of which China (P.R.C.) and India are the most prominent; and to meet the current serious threats to Western interests, especially in the Middle East, when these threats often seem to ordinary citizens more remote, abstract, and complex than during the Cold War. This daunting effort will clearly require transatlantic policies that involve a delicate and flexible combination of incentives and disincentives applied to these other countries in a highly discriminating manner in widely differing circumstances. Designing and sustaining such policies will be no easy task for Western governments with compelling domestic preoccupations in the full glare of the media spotlight.

During the Soviet era, both sides of the Atlantic were naturally focused almost entirely on threat assessment. To continue with that approach to international relations in the period ahead would ignore the powerful trends around the globe toward democracy and market economies that promise to continue to enlarge the core of democratic nations. (Bureaucracies tend to concentrate on caution and avoiding current catastrophes; statesmen construct to shape the future.) This is not to say that there are no serious dangers to Western interests as we approach the next century. As this report stresses, there are such threats and in the greater Middle East they are getting substantially worse. However, that disturbing part of the picture should not distort the fact that Western values and institutions are increasingly attractive the world over and can become progressively more so.

As this report goes to press in early 1999, transatlantic relations are on an even keel. Although Suez demonstrated in 1956 that sudden policy differences could fundamentally disrupt the alliance almost overnight, and while the Asian economic crises and the chaos in Russia continue to worry the United States and Europe deeply, there are currently no serious disputes across the Atlantic and none on the horizon. Indeed, the transatlantic partnership can be proud that in recent years it has ejected Iraq from Kuwait; stopped the killing in Bosnia; projected stability and democracy eastward through the enlargement of NATO to Poland, the Czech Republic, and Hungary; intensified a parallel stabilizing enlargement process within the European Union (EU); made extraordinary progress in Northern Ireland; managed security relations with Russia, at least this far, without a serious blowup; and—despite the current Asian and global economic dislocations—together produced a new burst of transatlantic mergers, acquisitions, and investments and led the struggle to open up further the international trading system.

To be sure, this is not a picture of perfect harmony and effective cooperation. Tactical disagreements on one subject or another come on to the primary transatlantic agenda from time to time; are managed, deferred, forgotten, or overtaken by events or changes in policy; and then go off the major operational list—often to appear again later. This has applied in recent years to the Middle East peace process, Western interaction with Turkey, relations with Iran and to a lesser degree Iraq, several disputatious bilateral trade issues, and so forth. But given that at the beginning of this decade some experts were predicting that the U.S.-European alliance would go to the grave along with the Cold War, this fundamental positive equilibrium in relations between the United States and Europe at present can be rightly seen as a major accomplishment by transatlantic governments.

Why has this been so? After all, only a few years ago the numbing cliché was frequently repeated that the glue holding the alliance together would dissolve with the demise of the Soviet Union, as would transatlantic policy collaboration. The argument went that without the Red Army menacing the center of the continent, Western Europe and the United States would fall into an endless series of policy conflicts and that this destructive process would gradually erode the very center of transatlantic cooperation. There are several reasons why this has not happened and why the doomsayers have been wrong.

First, American and European vital and important interests are largely identical and—equally acute—are so perceived by governments, dominant elites, and publics. Both sides of the Atlantic recognize that they have vital or important interests in slowing the spread of weapons of mass destruction; avoiding the emergence of a hostile hegemon in Europe; moving steadily toward a Europe that is whole, free, prosperous, and at peace; maintaining the secure supply of imported energy at reasonable prices; further opening up the transatlantic and global economic systems; and preventing the catastrophic collapse of international financial, trade, and ecological regimes.

In no instances do the United States and Europe have conflicting vital or important external interests. This congruency gives transatlantic governments every practical reason to search for ways to cooperate to exploit opportunities to advance these interests and to work together to meet serious threats to them. Although there will, of course, be frequent tactical disagreements across the Atlantic regarding how best to do this, the alliance agrees on these fundamentals that have nothing to do with deterring the Soviet Army in the center of a divided Germany. In addition, the two sides of the Atlantic share history, cultural affinity, and moral values that make the transatlantic partnership unique in the world.

With this as background and introduction, two broad prospective questions make up the bulk of this prescriptive report on the future of U.S.-European relations. Within Europe, how can the largely positive trends on the continent be maintained and through which transatlantic policies? And what improvements can be made in U.S.-European strategic cooperation outside Europe?

It is this latter question that clouds otherwise good prospects for the transatlantic relationship in the next decade. For none of the global U.S. vital interests enumerated above are presently threatened in Europe, except for the dangers associated with the safety and security of the Russian nuclear arsenal. This is entirely good news. After 70 years of the Nazi and then the Soviet military threat to Europe, because of the end of the Cold War and of the U.S.S.R. itself, American vital interests related to Europe are not presently in any serious danger, except with respect to Russian "loose nukes."

With U.S. vital interests connected to Europe relatively safe for the foreseeable future, Washington's security preoccupations are turning more and more toward those regions where vital American interests are threatened—most particularly in the greater Middle East and, to a lesser and more potential degree, in the Asia-Pacific region. In these crucial areas, the state of transatlantic cooperation is far less bright than on the continent. In the greater Middle East, the two sides of the Atlantic differ on the tactics for dealing with virtually every issue in the region: the Israel-Palestinian peace process; Western interaction with Iran; how best to slow proliferation of weapons of mass destruction into the area; the role of force in defending transatlantic interests in the region; and increasingly, even how best to deal with Saddam Hussein over the longer term. As for Western security challenges in Asia, including managing the rise of Chinese power, instability on the Korean peninsula, and the growing importance of India, the Europeans are virtually absent in any strategic sense.

These issues regarding transatlantic collaboration outside of Europe could again raise traditional burden-sharing problems across the Atlantic. The question is how long the Americans will accept that European security is a joint U.S.-European endeavor with Washington in the lead, while protecting transatlantic vital interests beyond the continent falls disproportionately to the United States. This is especially relevant on this side of the Atlantic because the task of defending Western interests in the world in the next decade and thereafter will exceed American economic means and national political will. Therefore, the

United States needs active partners. This report examines whether the present unbalanced division of labor between the United States and Europe can be sustained and whether it will adequately protect vital and important Western interests in the greater Middle East and in the Asia-Pacific region for the next ten years and beyond. "Doubtful" is the essential and troubling answer to these questions. And at best increased European involvement with the United States in meeting global security challenges is likely to be slow and incremental.

II. THE DOMESTIC CONTEXTS OF TRANSATLANTIC RELATIONS

Recent years have produced an increase in national domestic preoccupations throughout the industrial democracies. This is not necessarily a reason for unconstrained melancholy. With the end of the Soviet threat, governments and citizens are right to recognize that this is a period in which the sharp reduction of classical external security threats permits them to concentrate more than in most of this century on the challenging tasks of reforming and revitalizing their societies. Politicians and voters have become more inward-looking and less disposed to commit substantially to foreign endeavors, especially if they may be costly. Their willingness to take seriously calls from national security elites to engage in long-term strategic thinking or action is equally restrained. This is certainly true of publics in both Western Europe and the United States and is likely to remain so for the foreseeable future in the absence of a major external event that folks believe affects their personal lives and prospects. Transatlantic governments are importantly limited by these domestic factors as they attempt to cooperate to defend their national interests, to meet proximate threats, and to try to shape the international environment for the new millennium.

In Europe, politicians and public opinion are largely self-absorbed by a range of national problems: stimulating economic growth, lowering unemployment, downsizing the welfare state, dealing with the consequences of an aging population, ensuring adequate health care, combating crime, and reducing drug use. (Many of the European policy responses to these challenges seem increasingly borrowed from across the North Sea and the Atlantic.) All these problems are properly matters of debate in the parliaments and in other public discourse within the nations of the European Union and in EU bodies themselves. Most of whatever energy, resources, and political will that remains within the EU apart from these domestic tasks is devoted to the important efforts of Brussels to implement Economic and Monetary Union (EMU) successfully, to reform the internal decision-making structures and practices of the Union, to stabilize east central Europe through EU enlargement, and, most fundamentally, to construct a "Community of Fate" among Union members.

All this means that Europe's willingness and perhaps even capacity to join with the United States in dealing in any strategic and comprehensive way with the challenges and opportunities of the international system apart from those on or near the continent in the next five years may be modest. In some sense, this is understandable. Both EMU and EU enlargement remain unfinished tasks. Both could go quite wrong without continuing concentrated attention from Europe's heads of government, senior civil servants, and to a lesser extent, parliaments. At the same time, as we shall see throughout this report, such absorption by Western Europe with its own immediate problems and vicinity does leave managing most of the world's other international security responsibilities primarily to the United States, often with minimum assistance from America's European Allies.

This is especially true with respect to the instinctive hesitancy of most European countries, except for Britain and to a lesser degree France, to join the United States in the threat or use of force outside the continent to meet serious dangers to vital Western interests. With their almost exclusive emphasis on nonmilitary instruments to deal with virtually every international security problem, allied timidity with respect to the use of force will be a persistent problem for America and for the transatlantic alliance in the period ahead. Nothing less is required on the part of the

Europeans than to create, with American assistance as desired, a new post-Cold War strategic culture for the nations of the European Union that is consistent with the global security challenges facing the West in the next decade.

This brings us to the United States, which has also been going through its most insular period in more than 60 years. There are good reasons for this. The United States as a society is safer and more content than in many decades. There is no present competitor to American global leadership and probably none on the horizon for the next decade or more. Serious security threats to U.S. vital interests are at present confined, except on the Korean peninsula, to the proliferation of weapons of mass destruction into the hands of America's enemies, either rogue nations or nonstate actors, and to international grand terrorism. The U.S. domestic economy has been fundamentally sound and performing well for seven years, even so far in the face of the global consequences of the economic crises in Asia and beyond.

This relatively benign external situation has permitted most Americans, including the political class, to center their attention on the many challenges that confront U.S. society: the state of the economy, education, crime, drug abuse, health care, and welfare reform. In addition, many other issues have been driven from public scrutiny in 1998 by the domestic scandal engulfing the White House and questions related to the legal ramifications of President Clinton's actions and statements regarding his personal behavior. All this has meant that foreign policy concerns are not of much day-to-day interest to most Americans (the domestic effects of economic globalization and international terrorism are sometimes exceptions). More than anything else, this explains why the U.S. media are so domestically oriented, and why coverage of foreign affairs is now so limited, indeed poor, in the United States.

Every opinion poll shows that U.S. citizens, like their European counterparts, want their government to concentrate primarily on the nation's domestic problems. This does not mean that there is a new wave of isolationism on this side of the Atlantic. The U.S. public recognizes that American interests are ever more entwined with the international system, particularly with regard to the country's economic prosperity. It is noteworthy that despite the end of the Soviet threat and changing demographic patterns in the United States, the percentage of Americans today who believe that the United States should maintain or increase its commitment to NATO is a strong 64 percent, compared with 70 percent in 1986. U.S. citizens do appear to be willing to support in principle a leading U.S. diplomatic and military stance in the world. (Polling suggests that 73 percent of Americans believe that the United States will play a greater international role in the next ten years than it does at present.)

Concurrently, Americans are very cautious about Washington's leadership and activism in the world if it brings with it a heavy price for the United States, either in blood or in treasure. To put it differently, the U.S. public seems willing to allow its government to engage vigorously in the world as long as it does not get into trouble in regions or on issues that are not vital to the United States, and if the burden of this international activism—and this is a crucial point—is fairly shared over time by others, especially America's allies. At the same time, as we saw in 1993 in Somalia and in 1982 in Lebanon, sharp international reversals, particularly in situations not connected to vital or important American interests, can cause the United States to pull back in a spasm from overseas involvements, with or without the allies.

The general lack of curiosity about events abroad on the part of the U.S. public produces a situation in which special interest groups and one-issue lobbies have more influence on U.S. foreign policy than ever before. And most of these groups, whether they concentrate on human rights, abortion, environmental matters, or the concerns of various ethnic diasporas, have no particular connection to the Atlantic relationship. (Business lobbies with a transatlantic perspective are an important exception to this trend.) Thus, when inevitable disputes arise across the Atlantic on individual issues, these interest groups are often likely to have more influence in Congress—a Congress less attentive to foreign affairs than any since the late 1930s—than do more general calls for transatlantic solidarity on behalf of broader regional and global purposes. This, in part, explains the inclination of some in

Congress instinctively to want to punish our allies through sanctions when they do not agree with the direction or details of U.S. policy.

These domestic factors, as well as a sustained U.S. difficulty in dealing with the new geopolitical situation, have in recent years sometimes led to a problem of inconstancy in American policy. The allies can hardly be expected to back U.S. policies if they are not sure such policies will be in place tomorrow or the next day. There is thus a palpable worry in European capitals that on any particular issue, Washington may well change its mind overnight and, without consultation, leave the allies in the lurch or retreat because of domestic scandal from its international leadership responsibilities, at least for a time. The past few years have also seen occasional triumphalist attitudes emanating from Washington that are arrogant, self-righteous, and not backed up by U.S. action and resources everywhere they are needed, and that harmfully feed the psychology of dependence among the allies.

In virtually the same moment, one often hears wails of American frustration that its transcendent power does not seem to mean that it can get its way quickly in the world, or sometimes at all. This U.S. frustration occasionally leads to unilateral American action that, while in certain instances the only realistic U.S. recourse, generally makes it more difficult for European governments to support the United States even when they agree. In the long run, it is this temptation in Washington to act without the allies—not American isolationism, which every poll shows is quite unlikely—that will cause the most difficulties from the U.S. side in the transatlantic relationship. With respect to its European allies, Washington does not consult enough; it does not listen enough; it does not respect the views of the allies enough (good ideas are not invented only in Washington); and it does not sufficiently acknowledge allied contributions to international peace and stability (including European financial contributions to the United Nations, the International Monetary Fund [IMF], and other international organizations).

These domestic preoccupations on the two sides of the Atlantic, along with the adjustment of their traditional working democracies to globalization and its effects, do not make robust U.S.-European cooperation easy. Nevertheless, as is indicated in this report, there are numerous examples in recent years of successful transatlantic collaboration on behalf of common interests and international peace and security. But these factors, along with the fact that the U.S.-European relationship is based less these days on emotion and sentiment and more on perceptions of national interests, do suggest that parliaments and publics in both Europe and the United States are less inclined to think in a transatlantic context than during the five decades of the Soviet global threat.

III. EUROPEAN SECURITY AND POLITICAL ECONOMY

The core of U.S.-European relations will remain the transatlantic ability to cooperate on issues related to Europe from the Atlantic to the Urals. Led by the United States as a European power, success in that respect will not necessarily produce broader collaboration in the global system. But failure to work closely together to promote stability in Europe would probably fatally undermine the possibility for comprehensive joint action elsewhere. Moreover, Europe's first preoccupation is, and should be, the promotion of stability on the continent. If Europe is seriously unstable, there will be little or no chance that the allies will be prepared over the longer term to look beyond Europe to a broad partnership with the United States to lead in the management of global international security and political economy. So increased peace and security in Europe through intense U.S.-European cooperation is a sine qua non for further extending those benign European conditions and successful transatlantic comity into the rest of the world, especially the greater Middle East and East Asia. And the situation in Europe in recent years is mostly good, particularly when compared with the past several hundred years.

This matters a great deal because the United States retains—as it has most of this century—vital and important national interests vis-à-vis Europe writ large:

- To prevent a hostile hegemon from again threatening European peace and security;

- To ensure that there is no proliferation of weapons of mass destruction (WMD) into or from Europe;

- To help ensure the safety and security of the Russian nuclear arsenal;

- To interact economically with Europe in ways that increase U.S. wealth and prosperity;

- To support the continuation of European integration consistent with American interests;

- To export democracy, prosperity, and stability eastward on the continent;

- To do what is possible to continue to support democratic institutions and market practices in Russia;

- Most fundamental of all, to ensure that never again do the major powers of Western Europe return to the tragic rivalries of the past.

NO HOSTILE HEGEMON

The good news is that these U.S. national interests are for the most part not seriously threatened. The demise of the Soviet Union and the current extraordinary weakness of Russia—the only plausible candidate for a country with a dominating continental appetite—means that the emergence of a hostile hegemonic threat to Europe appears quite unlikely for at least 15 to 20 years at the earliest.

WEAPONS OF MASS DESTRUCTION

There is also no sign at present that any nonnuclear nation in Europe aspires to acquire weapons of mass destruction. With respect to the allied export of sensitive technologies to important and unstable regions of the world, the European performance has improved markedly in recent years. EU export controls in this regard are now nearly as rigorous as those of the United States, another significant transatlantic accomplishment. As is indicated in the next section of this report concerning the greater Middle East, a crucial U.S.-European challenge for the period ahead, which is not now satisfactorily being met, will be to develop compatible strategies for dealing with miscreant states and criminal nonstate actors seeking to acquire weapons of mass destruction, notably in areas of the world that matter a great deal to the transatlantic community.

U.S.-European cooperation with respect to safeguarding the Russian WMD arsenal also needs improvement. On the nuclear side, this entails 7,000 Russian nuclear warheads mounted on strategic missiles capable of reaching the United States; 5,000 tactical nuclear weapons; and 70,000 nuclear weapons equivalents in stockpiles of highly enriched uranium and plutonium. This is a problem on which the United States has spent a good deal of time, energy, and money since the early 1990s. The U.S. accomplishment in persuading Ukraine, Belarus, and Kazakhstan to give up the nuclear weapons on their soil after 1991 was one of the singular American diplomatic accomplishments of recent decades. And through the inventive Nunn-Lugar program, Washington has devoted about $400 million annually to try to minimize this danger. In sharp contrast, the allies have basically ignored this issue. Although there are minimalist EU efforts in play, the European political classes and publics either do not take this threat seriously or believe that the United States will deal with it satisfactorily.

The meltdown of Russia's political and economic structures in mid-1998, along with the fact that most elements of the Russian armed forces, including the nuclear forces, do not receive regular salaries, should set off warning sirens all over Europe. Curiously, this does not seem to have happened. From an American perspective, such indifference on the part of the allies is deeply worrisome because the danger of a transfer of "loose nukes" as well as chemical and biological weapons from the Russian arsenal to enemies of the United States and Europe in the Middle East and Persian Gulf is the only serious threat to U.S. vital interests emanating from

Europe for the foreseeable future. Early Duma ratification of the START II Treaty and a swift continuation into START III negotiations would also make an important contribution to meeting this challenge.

A EUROPE WHOLE AND FREE

The European Union is now playing an indispensable role in exporting stability to the eastern side of the continent. The EU decision to open membership negotiations with the six "fast-track" countries of Poland, the Czech Republic, Hungary, Estonia, Slovenia, and Cyprus, and the consequent intense daily interaction this entails between the institutions in Brussels and these nations, is one of the strategic reasons why U.S. interests in Europe are thriving. Moreover, prospective EU membership for those applicant countries that are not in this current enlargement tranche provides considerable incentives for them to move persistently along the pluralist and free-market paths.

Some American experts and many in EU candidate countries are critical of what they regard as the slow pace of the Union's enlargement. In turn, EU politicians and officials stress the extraordinary technical complexity and difficulty of these membership negotiations and upon occasion irritably dismiss these U.S. reproaches, reminding Americans that getting EU enlargement done right is more important than getting it done quickly. Most Americans probably underestimate the economic equities and thus the domestic political sensitivities at stake for EU member states in the enlargement process. At the same time, EU officials sometimes give the impression that highly technical economic details are entirely driving the pace of EU enlargement, and that the strategic importance of this historic process to Europe and to the United States does not play a sufficiently important part in the calculations of Brussels. Thus, it is probably right for Washington to keep up the pressure on its allies to move the next phase of enlargement along as rapidly as possible while recognizing that U.S. opinions will

remain on the margins of EU decision-making on this complicated subject.

With respect to Economic and Monetary Union in January 1999,
there is a debate across the Atlantic regarding the consequences
for transatlantic relations of this action on the part of 11 EU
countries. Critics argue that the economies of the EU are too diverse
and at different stages of growth for EMU to work well; that weak-
nesses in labor mobility, differing cultures and languages, and
the absence of an adequate and systematic mechanism for fiscal
transfers to countries and regions that may suffer from EMU will
undermine the idea's implementation; that EMU will further
worsen unemployment, raise interest rates, impede growth, and
decrease Europe's fiscal flexibility; that Europe's banks and companies remain unprepared for the Euro; that EMU will create a
two-tier Europe; that the EMU process will distract Europe from
developing a common foreign and security policy, modernizing
Europe's defenses, and joining the United States in managing global security; that the Euro will quickly join the dollar in a bipolar
currency regime and increasingly compete with the dollar for
international investment; and that EMU will cause Europe to become more protectionist and thus weaken transatlantic and perhaps even global trade. This is quite a list.

While it is certainly true that EMU carries with it significant
risks, that it could go disastrously aground, and that it will
undoubtedly encounter many bumps along the way, the overall ana-
lytic balance regarding transatlantic relations is decisively in favor
of economic and monetary union. It will lower transactional costs
that will save both money and time for European individuals
and businesses. It will eliminate exchange-rate volatility within the
EMU zone. It will likely foster fiscal discipline and help keep inflation rates low among EMU nations. It will unleash the full potential of the EU single market and thus stimulate economic growth
and wealth creation in Europe. It will bring about big new opportunities for American businesses. It will not produce a plausible
reserve currency to challenge the dollar for many, many years, if
then. And, perhaps most important of all, it will create a stronger
European Union with greater economic, political, and social

cohesion. Thus, the United States should worry not that EMU will succeed but that it could fail.

Although by no means guaranteed, this EMU process could also over time promote enhanced cooperation and coordination between the European Union and the United States in economic, security, and diplomatic matters. If EMU is successful and Europe's economic growth increases, it will in addition be good for American exports, and therefore for the U.S. economy and U.S. businesses. Having come down firmly on the side of economic and monetary union in this report, it is also important to stress that it will bring new challenges to U.S.-European policy interaction. Although it has been the conventional wisdom during the past five decades that both Europe and the United States can only benefit from the strengthening of the other, the allies wonder on occasion whether this is really true with America as the sole superpower. In the same way, the new and emerging organization of Europe does not automatically mean a boost for America and closer transatlantic collaboration and burden sharing. It is possible for the EU to integrate further and at the same time to decline to share equitably international responsibilities with the United States. And if representatives of a more integrated EU deal with the United States in a bureaucratic manner reflecting a rigid Union consensus, this would be a recipe for enduring problems across the Atlantic. The model for U.S.-EU strategic collaboration in the long run should be U.S.-U.K. policy interchange, which is usually marked by transparency, candor, and mutual respect.

The final transatlantic issue with respect to the European Union is the EU's relationship with Turkey. There seems little reason for U.S. sympathy for the Union's distressing approach to this significant NATO ally and Western asset. Turkey is located on a critically important strategic intersection, facing as it does the Persian Gulf, the Caucasus and the Caspian basin, and southeastern Europe. Imagine the geopolitical consequences for the transatlantic community if Turkey were to lose Atatürk's secular orientation and become a destabilizing nation animated by the aims of aggressive political Islam. That would be a disaster for Western interests in all three regions that Turkey abuts.

Yet although the European Union proudly and rightly proclaims its intensifying mission into east central Europe, its policies toward Ankara often ignore Turkey's strategic importance in favor of a hectoring and even arrogant approach to this NATO ally that was so faithful throughout the 40 years of confrontation with the Soviet Union. Why does the EU not have an equally intense desire to project stability into Turkey? The Turks often answer that it is their Muslim faith that leads Europeans to be hypercritical of the Turkish government's problems with human rights and its Kurdish minority. It is difficult to argue that this is completely wrong. At the same time, EU members are right to stress the many structural economic difficulties and political challenges that prevent Turkey's early entry into the Union. (In this respect, it is counterproductive for Americans to call for rapid Turkish membership in the Union; that will not happen and such statements further damage relations between Brussels and Ankara.) Furthermore, the Turkish minorities in Union member states, notably in Germany, generate domestic political opposition to improved relations with Ankara. And Greece makes any EU moves toward Turkey exceedingly hard to accomplish.

For all these reasons, the transatlantic interest of projecting stability eastward on the continent is not being successfully implemented with respect to Turkey. As is demonstrated by Italy's misguided handling of the capture of Kurdish guerrilla leader Abdullah Ocalan, quite the contrary. This does not mean that the United States and its European allies should ignore the problems in Turkey related to human rights, the rule of law, and treatment of minorities. Constant subtle pressure on Turkey in these respects should be a major element of U.S.-European policies. This should occur, however, in an environment in which it is made clear to the Turkish elite and general populace that Western Europe and the United States regard Turkey as "one of us," a longtime ally and friend.

Unlike policy toward Turkey, the successful reform of the North Atlantic Alliance in recent years and its preeminent role in exporting stability eastward in Europe has been a striking example of consummate transatlantic cooperation and another preeminent reason why U.S. vital and important national interests in Europe are being skillfully promoted.

This superb alliance record has been evidenced most importantly in NATO enlargement to include Poland, the Czech Republic, and Hungary; in NATO's noble if belated effort to stop the killing in Bosnia; in the alliance's largely unsung achievement through the Partnership for Peace in strengthening ties and promoting security reform in the dozens of countries east and south of Poland that will not be NATO members in the near future; and in the alliance's conceptual attempt to bring Russia closer to the center of NATO decision-making regarding the current and prospective challenges of European security.

This splendid record did not happen by accident. It was the sustained and systematic result of enlightened and collaborative policies by governments on both sides of the Atlantic, led by the United States. Thus, the questions of the early 1990s concerning the relevance of the alliance in the present era have been answered decisively. The deeply reformed NATO is the indispensable hub of the post-Cold War European security system.

This does not mean, however, that NATO can be complacent as it shapes its role in Europe in the period ahead. With respect to both NATO enlargement and the Balkans, trouble may well lie ahead for U.S.-European relations and for the continent. Conceptually, the alliance cannot now retreat from its open-door policy with respect to new members. But inviting any other nation to join NATO in the next three to five years would be unwise. It is exactly during this period that NATO should be considering its future strategic orientation. No additional nations should be offered membership in the alliance before that prolonged analytical and prescriptive process is completed. In addition, NATO needs to digest carefully the entry of the three new members in 1999 to ensure that its decision-making in routine and crisis situations can be maintained. We must not turn the most successful alliance in world history into a debating club through rapid expansion. Finally, but less important, NATO should take into account Russia's attitude to further enlargement as the alliance decides the pace of expansion.

If the alliance were to proceed with an early round of enlargement, such a decision would probably further weaken practical concerted action between NATO and the Russian Federation. Although this collaborative interaction is thus far mostly only on paper, the alliance should persist in attempting to draw Moscow responsibly into the management of European security. This will be very difficult to accomplish given the chaos in Russia and its instinctive opposition to transatlantic security objectives in Europe and almost everywhere else. Nonetheless, NATO should persevere in looking for responsible ways to take account of Russian perspectives on European security, as long as the essential missions and values of the alliance are not compromised. (There seems to have been some progress in this respect at the December 9, 1998, meeting of NATO's Permanent Joint Council.) This is a key part of the transatlantic effort to help bring long-term peace and stability to all of Europe from the Atlantic to the Urals.

The Balkans also present important challenges for NATO, both real and potential. This is a situation in which European vital interests are at stake because of the region's proximity, while vital or important American interests are not directly engaged in this particular piece of real estate. Nevertheless, the United States should be a major participant in NATO's stabilizing effort in Bosnia. With European political will to act in combat situations without the United States at its usual low ebb, Washington's failure to become involved on the ground in Bosnia would probably have produced a continuing bloody, and perhaps spreading, disaster in the Balkans. This, in turn, would have overly preoccupied the European political scene; made it less likely that the allies would have been available for the many other important tasks of European security (not to say the challenges outside the continent); and deeply undermined the relevance and effectiveness of NATO at a critical time after the Cold War. So although American national interests are not directly connected to the future of the Balkans, they are fundamentally entwined with NATO's health and the allied capability and willingness to join the United States in the broader challenges of international security. This is a realpolitik answer to those who ask why

U.S. forces should intervene in Bosnia to reduce human suffering but not in many other places in the world.

Alliance military policy in Bosnia has been brilliantly executed since the summer of 1995. Because of the tranquilizing presence of U.S. and allied military forces, the killing has been stopped in Bosnia and the ethnic cleansing there has been slowed dramatically. On the political side in Bosnia, the West's policies have been much less effective and they may well be based on a faulty premise, i.e., that the three communities can be brought to regard themselves as integral parts of one country. As the September 1998 elections in Bosnia may have demonstrated, this might turn out to be too difficult a task for outsiders to accomplish. Nevertheless, NATO, the European Union, and the international community should continue to try for a broad political outcome in Bosnia because the alternative could be communal pressures to resume the conflict. In any case, NATO forces, including those of the United States, should remain on the ground in Bosnia for years to come. Given the bloody and destabilizing alternatives, this is a cost-effective way to expend alliance resources. Thus, there should be no NATO and no U.S. exit strategy from Bosnia. To formulate one would increase substantially the likelihood that the fighting would break out again. In short, NATO security policy in Bosnia is working well. Let us not try to fix it.

Kosovo is another matter. At present and in light of the October 13, 1998, deal brokered by Richard Holbrooke, Yugoslav President Slobodan Milosevic may again intend to skillfully outmaneuver the West, as he did during the early years of the Bosnian crisis. Time will tell. In any case, with the alliance hesitant to become militarily involved in a complicated Balkan ethnic dispute, Milosevic was free to employ brutal force in Kosovo for over six months—destroying villages, producing again an untold number of civilian deaths at Serbian hands, and causing hundreds of thousands of refugees to take to the roads. In the fall of 1998, with the Balkan winter approaching, NATO finally began making preparations to intervene to stop the conflict, and by early October, air strikes seemed imminent. To avert such action, Milosevic agreed to end the crackdown, significantly reduce Serb forces in

Kosovo, begin negotiations with ethnic Albanians on a political settlement to the crisis, and permit the stationing of 2,000 international monitors on the ground and NATO reconnaissance flights. Nevertheless, at this writing, Milosevic's compliance with the terms of this agreement seems quite uncertain and the two sides seem to be preparing for war in the spring of 1999. As U.S. envoy Richard Holbrooke warned in mid-December, the warring sides in Kosovo are "playing with dynamite." Complicated issues of self-determination for the Kosovars are a critical part of any eventual solution. But with the armed resistance in Kosovo gaining increasing political influence, there will be no easy answer to the ultimate division of power between Belgrade and Pristina.

What is not tolerable is for the transatlantic community to stand aside militarily while ethnic conflict again engulfs southeastern Europe and Milosevic again systematically brutalizes massive numbers of innocents. As with Bosnia, the southern Balkans must be tranquilized, with or without U.N. Security Council authorization, to provide a secure European pillar to transatlantic collaboration in the next century. That is the fundamental reason why the two sides of the Atlantic should be decisive in ending for good the conflict in Kosovo and why America should be centrally engaged in this endeavor.

Some on this side of the Atlantic will wonder why the allies cannot take care of Bosnia and Kosovo without U.S. leadership and direct military involvement. Given the security challenges that America faces in the Middle East and in East Asia for the next decade and beyond, the United States would certainly benefit if Europe were to play a larger role in solving the continent's security problems up to the eastern Polish border. This is why Washington should support the concept of a European security and defense identity, including the early December 1998 initiative by Britain and France, as long as it is backed up by actual modernized military capability and harnessed to transatlantic security objectives. The problem here is not the decline of European military capabilities but their unsuitability. U.S. forces have shrunk more than European forces since the end of the Cold War, and the American defense budget has declined as much as those of the allies. But the United States is putting its resources and investments generally into modernizing military forces, while the allies, except for the United Kingdom, are spending far too much to maintain obsolescent forces. If these trends continue and Europe falls even further behind in the revolution in military affairs, at some point in the not-too-distant future the two sides of the Atlantic will not be capable of effectively going to war together. To close this growing gap will require cross-Atlantic defense industry investment and a free market in the information technologies on which new defense systems are based.

Such an increased allied component in European security and enhanced European weight in transatlantic decision-making related to the continent will produce some heartburn in Washington from time to time. But this somewhat reduced U.S. security influence and exposure in Europe would be consistent both with increased transatlantic burden sharing and with American security responsibilities in the rest of the world. In the end, however, only the Europeans can make this happen, and regrettably they seem to be producing little progress at present.

A more tolerant, even supportive, U.S. approach with respect to growing allied influence on matters of European security does involve some changes. It should not encourage the Europeans to become even more preoccupied with their own concerns on the continent at the expense of an increasing partnership with the United States to shape the international system in the new era. Here, NATO's new Strategic Concept, which will be adopted at the April 1999 Washington summit, becomes acutely relevant. That document should capture the current strategic actualities facing the West as it approaches the next century: a Europe that is progressing well in a security sense but with work still to be done; a Russia that will probably be problematic for the transatlantic community for decades to come; and crucially, a set of security challenges outside of Europe, especially in the Middle East, that are likely increasingly to threaten Western vital interests in the years ahead. (Any effort in this context by the new German government to push for a NATO no-first-use policy regarding nuclear weapons would be seriously wrongheaded.) If NATO is not relevant to security challenges outside Europe, the United States may over time drift somewhat away from its central alliance vocation in favor of other instruments to promote and protect its vital interests. To put it in a more positive way, NATO's integrated military structure is the only serious transatlantic instrument for detailed joint military planning, and it should progressively be used to plan for all security threats to vital and important transatlantic interests. Although this will not happen overnight, NATO should accelerate the process. Secretary of State Madeleine Albright's speech in this respect at the December 8, 1998, NATO Ministerial meeting was a step in the right direction. But as the tepid or worse allied reaction on that occasion showed, Washington will have to keep its mind centrally on this subject for months and years to come.

RUSSIA

Impossible as it is to capture in print in any enduring way the twists and turns of that enormous country and its current profound time of troubles, there are some fundamental points to be made regarding transatlantic policy toward the Russian Federation. First, it is difficult to see much else the West could have done in the past few years to try to promote the emergence in Russia of a genuine market economy. There may have been an opportunity in the early 1990s to drive a highly conditional Grand Bargain with the new Russia and a vigorous Boris Yeltsin in which far greater Western resources would have been committed over a shorter time period to promote and ease the Russian political and economic transition. But that may well not have worked either because of the same internal Russian political and societal dynamics that have produced the current crisis.

In any event, in recent years the United States and Europe have constantly faced the same dilemma with respect to policy toward Russia. Since 1993, the IMF could try as it might to exact from Moscow the most stringent possible conditions regarding tight budgets, low inflation, wage arrears, tax collection, implementing fair privatization, breaking up monopolies, and so forth, tied to segmented tranches of IMF loans. But Western governments could never in the end permit those negotiations to fail. To do so could have set Russia on the nightmarish path of the disintegration of a nuclear superpower. So Russian economic reform over this period was always halting, hesitant—too little, too late, and never supported by the Russian Duma.

That these Western economic efforts did not produce success in Russia and that the August 17, 1998, economic meltdown occurred should not be cause for the donning of transatlantic hair shirts, especially given the effects on Russia of a 50 percent fall in the price of oil, the Asian financial crises, the deep incompetence of the Yeltsin government, and the growing infirmity of Yeltsin himself. There are some public policy problems that turn out simply to be too hard. The United States and Europe did what they could but that rightly did not include trying to take over Russia and force domestic economic reforms on the country. In the final analysis, Russia is responsible for its current calamities because of the failure of its political institutions and public morality, and only the Russian political process can find a way out. Given the very low support for reform among the Russian populace (15 percent or less), one cannot be very optimistic in the short to medium term.

This does not mean that the Western effort was flawless. While doing what they could to support Russia's economic transformation, the United States and Europe should have devoted many more resources to helping develop democratic institutions in the federation. Such an effort would have entailed a fraction of the money that was devoted to the economic side and would have given political reformers in Russia more of a chance to overcome the negative shadows of the country's one-thousand-year history. Curiously, the West instead concentrated almost entirely on an approach that seemed to imagine that economic factors would produce benign and democratic political outcomes in Russia.

What now? When this report is published in early 1999, as demonstrated in the assassination in late October 1998 of liberal reformer Galina Starovoitova, virtually any outcome is possible in the coming months. But whatever the trend of events there (and they are highly unlikely to be positive), the transatlantic community should not disengage. The safety and security of Russia's enormous nuclear arsenal in particular would make such U.S.-European disconnection extremely unwise. Imagine a Russian government so enfeebled that it could not prevent the sale of nuclear, chemical, and biological materials and/or weapons as well as even more advanced missile technologies to the Middle East. Or imagine a Russian government so hostile to the United States and other Western nations that it decided to transfer weapons-grade nuclear, chemical, or biological material or even the weapons themselves and perhaps the missiles to carry them to these rogue states and/or nonstate actors.

So the transatlantic community must continue to struggle to help a Russia whose own actions make the success of such assistance extremely questionable. The West should continue to stress that it will resume IMF loans to Russia and reschedule Russia's foreign debt if Moscow takes decisive steps to stabilize the economy through serious reforms and to restore investor confidence, with the concurrence of the Duma. If the Russian government does not proceed with these domestic economic reforms, if it seeks to deal with the present crisis principally by printing money (which would likely lead to hyperinflation), then there is nothing the transatlantic nations can or should do with resources to assist Russia through this crisis. In short, strategic patience is called for on the part of the United States and Europe, but it surely will not be easy to maintain. And while trying hard to forestall worst-case outcomes in Russia, both sides of the Atlantic should be prepared for them over the long term.

NO RETURN TO THE PAST

Finally, there is the U.S. national interest in ensuring that Western Europe does not again succumb to the bloody national rivalries of the past. America, with 100,000 troops in the European theater, remains the indispensable honest broker to ensure that the enormous gains of European integration in the past four decades are not reversed. It is in this most historic sense that economic and monetary union is important. EMU is, on balance, likely to bring more prosperity to Europe and to be a positive factor in the world economy. Americans should wish it well for those reasons alone. But most fundamentally, EMU is a further step in Western Europe's integration, a process that has deeply served U.S. national interests in the last 40 years.

PRESCRIPTIONS

- The greatest threat to vital transatlantic interests in Europe is the weak internal security surrounding Russia's nuclear weapons and material as well as its chemical and biological arsenal. While the United States is not doing enough to address this danger, the allies are doing almost nothing. This should urgently change; the Europeans should spend much more money on the problem.

- Washington, in conjunction with the Russian government, should move quickly to START III and further significant reductions when the Duma ratifies the START II Treaty.

- After the entry of Poland, the Czech Republic, and Hungary into NATO in 1999, there should be an informal pause for at least three to five years before any new candidates are invited to join the alliance.

- NATO should continue to strengthen its Partnership for Peace program, one of the most imaginative initiatives in alliance history.

- The alliance should try harder to find ways to take legitimate Russian security concerns into account and should strive to give more substance to the NATO-Russia Permanent Joint Council.

- Transatlantic support for Ukraine's independence and territorial integrity should be further enhanced.

- NATO should put an end to all military conflict in the Balkans and keep it that way.

- NATO forces, including U.S. troops on the ground, should remain in Bosnia to keep the peace for the foreseeable future and to try to create the conditions for a stable civil society.

- If Milosevic does not uphold his commitment to end the crackdown in Kosovo and begin serious negotiations toward a lasting political settlement, NATO should use all available means, including military force, to stop the violence against the Albanian majority. At the same time, the alliance should stand solidly against Kosovo independence; doing otherwise would reinforce dangerous precedents in the Balkans.

- NATO should conceptually broaden its new Strategic Concept to deal with threats to shared Western interests beyond Europe, especially in the Middle East: to protect Gulf oil, to slow the entry of weapons of mass destruction and missile delivery systems into that region, and to undertake the long-term joint military planning necessary to prepare for these contingencies. This strategic and operational evolution of NATO, which will not happen quickly, will require strong leadership from Washington over several years.

- The next phase of EU enlargement should proceed consistent with transatlantic strategic objectives regarding enhanced peace, democracy, prosperity, and stability on the continent. In particular, the Union should not bog down in the financial details of enlargement at the expense of the endeavor's geopolitical purpose.

- An intensification of the Union's common foreign and security policy can serve U.S. interests if it produces a more coherent Europe capable of playing a greater role in the world, and not a slide toward EU consensus at the lowest possible denominator, paralysis that could block national action by Europe's major powers, or even an instinct to define Europe's external identity at America's expense.

- Washington should also support the evolution of a European security and defense identity if it is within the transatlantic context and if it is accompanied by modernized European defense and power-projection capabilities.

- This will require a much intensified transatlantic effort in defense industry cooperation.

- Both the United States and Europe should work harder to help ensure Turkey's Western orientation.

- The European Union and its member states should try much harder to repair systematically their relationship with Ankara. The EU should make clear to Turkey that it has as much right to join the Union, when the Turks have met the necessary conditions, as any of the other applicants.

- Washington should stop calling for early EU membership for Turkey, a wholly unrealistic and unhelpful proposition at present.

- The United States should strongly support the EMU.

- Despite the current enormous difficulties inside Russia, the West should continue to do what it responsibly can to promote economic reform within the country, if the Russian government takes the necessary steps, and increase greatly its support for democratic institution building in Russia.

- If this combined cooperative effort between Russia and the West finally begins to work effectively over time, the transatlantic community should resume its efforts to further integrate Russia into international institutions.

- At the same time, the United States and Europe should prepare urgently on a contingency basis for the variety of bad outcomes in Russia that would threaten Western vital and important interests.

IV. THE TRANSATLANTIC RELATIONSHIP, THE GREATER MIDDLE EAST, AND ASIA

As indicated at length in the preceding section, U.S.-European collaboration regarding the challenges of the continent has been notably intense and successful in recent years. The same cannot be said for transatlantic efforts to exploit opportunities and deal with threats to Western interests emanating from the greater Middle East and from East and South Asia.

The principal and shorter-term worry in this respect relates to different perspectives and sometimes policies by the two sides of the Atlantic regarding most issues concerning the greater Middle East. Despite the obvious fact that Western interests related to securing access to energy at reasonable prices from the Gulf and slowing the flow of weapons of mass destruction into the region are increasingly threatened, the United States and Europe are often at odds on how best to protect these vital interests and meet these serious threats. (Washington would add to its interests in the greater Middle East protecting the safety and security of Israel, but it is not clear how high that interest actually ranks in European priorities for the region.)

THE TRANSATLANTIC MILITARY CHALLENGE

A fundamental challenge facing the United States and Europe over the next decade is to translate and transfer the extraordinary patterns of transatlantic cooperation that helped end the Cold War and have provided such a salutary boost to European stability in recent years to regions outside Europe, in the first instance to the Persian Gulf area. At present, it is almost solely America's military responsibility along with help from the United Kingdom on behalf of the West to secure the flow of energy from the Gulf and in parallel to take almost all the risks associated with that military protection. These risks include especially terrorism against Americans and U.S. facilities worldwide and growing threats from weapons of mass destruction to U.S. forces in the region and perhaps to the American homeland. Since Europe is far more dependent on imported oil from the Gulf than is the United States, this may not be a tenable division of labor over the long run in the view of American citizens. After all, why should their sons and daughters have to go into mortal danger in an area that is certainly at least as crucial to Europe as to the United States?

Answers from the other side of the Atlantic sometimes go something like this:

—"We prefer to concentrate on our historic task of stabilizing Europe at least for the next decade";

—"We don't do combat anymore; that's the U.S. specialty";

—"Our comparative advantage in Europe regarding the greater Middle East is in instruments of political economy, not of military force";

—"Our outdated military forces simply cannot get to the Gulf in a timely manner capable of rendering real assistance to the United States";

—"We cannot afford the resources required to create the sort of power projection capabilities that would allow us to join the United States in a major way in Gulf contingencies";

—"We rather like the current situation in which the United States takes almost all the risks concerning the Gulf and we Europeans, as free riders, reap the rewards; why would we want to change that?,"

—"Don't ask us to go fight in the Middle East as a result of the failure of U.S. policies, about which we were not consulted."

These European answers seem largely to suffice today in a Washington that has been drenched in preoccupying scandal and in a nation that is content and prosperous at this writing. However, this could change should events in the Gulf force the United States to go persistently into significant military combat almost entirely without its European allies, as it did at the end of 1998. If such intervention goes sour, causing considerable U.S. casualties, America at large could begin to ask why this patently unfair transatlantic military division of labor exists regarding protecting energy resources from the Gulf, especially since U.S. dependence on Gulf oil is declining. One could not dismiss the possibility in this circumstance of a precipitous U.S. military withdrawal from the Gulf region, leaving it mostly up to the allies to fend for themselves for the oil on which they so desperately depend. This would be a catastrophic outcome for all concerned on both sides of the Atlantic.

The United States needs genuine coalition partners as it seeks to manage this volatile and dangerous region, and the European allies are the only viable candidates. If they do not join the United States importantly in this endeavor, including participating when force is required as an instrument of deterrence or coercion, one could well expect increasing American unilateralism, as with the attacks on the Afghanistan terrorist camps and alleged Sudanese chemical weapons facility in the summer of 1998. As a consistent pattern of U.S. behavior, this would undermine transatlantic cooperation across the board and make it even less likely that the allies would join Washington in a comprehensive way to promote Western vital interests in the Middle East as recommended in this report.

This is not to argue in any way that military instruments are the answer to all, or even most, of the problems of the greater Middle East. That is certainly not so. The European Union has led the way in a manner Washington should emulate in tangibly recognizing the importance of economic assistance to the region to buttress moderate Arab regimes and to try to address the underlying causes of societal instability. Indeed, it is useful to remember that it was Norway that brokered the Oslo agreement and that the European Union provides the bulk of financial assistance to the Palestinian Authority. But integrated U.S.-European military action based on routine preparations across the Atlantic and usually securely connected to diplomatic action should be one feasible and ever ready (not just rhetorical) transatlantic instrument. This is why the European failure, except for Britain and to a lesser degree France, to modernize their force capabilities must be urgently reversed.

THE MIDDLE EAST PEACE PROCESS

Even if EU governments could be persuaded to proceed over the next several years to modernize their military forces and expand their geopolitical horizons in the way this report suggests, that would not remove the more pressing disagreements across the Atlantic regarding the most effective policies toward the region. Despite the progress in the Middle East peace process at Wye Plantation in October 1998, most Europeans believe that Washington as demonstrated through the rest of 1998 is not sufficiently tough on Israel when Jerusalem takes what the EU regards as unreasonable positions in negotiations with the Palestinians, and that American Middle East policy is overly influenced by U.S. domestic politics. As noted in general at the outset, there is no doubt that special interest groups have great influence on America's Middle East policies. This is an abiding characteristic of American democracy today and it is unlikely to be altered any time soon.

Nor is the close link in the minds of American presidential aspirants between their chances for success and their stance on U.S. policies on the peace process between Israel and the Palestinians going to change. Indeed, domestic political support for Israel is probably stronger among U.S. politicians, including in Congress, than at any time in many decades. Thus, although in recent years EU involvement in the real negotiations has increased a bit, the willingness of any U.S. administration to allow the Union to play anything approaching an equal role in the Middle East peace process is likely to remain quite limited. These U.S. domestic political inhibitions are reinforced by a perception in Washington that EU policy toward the peace process is sometimes overly influenced by European dependence on Arab oil and insufficiently sensitive to Israel's genuine security requirements and by the judgment of participants in the region that—despite the Oslo Accords—it is the United States that holds the external key to progress in the peace process. None of this is very new and, despite allied frustrations, U.S.-European cooperation regarding the Middle East peace process will have to work within these constraints.

Nevertheless, somewhat more balance between the two sides of the Atlantic regarding relations between Israel and its Arab neighbors is possible and desirable. Washington should quicken the trend toward using the EU as a reinforcing diplomatic instrument to support U.S. efforts; at the same time Washington needs to pay more attention with more resources to the underlying causes of instability within moderate Arab regimes. For its part, while responsibly importuning the United States to press Israel for more flexibility in the peace process, the European Union should tie its aid to the Palestinian Authority more directly to strenuous and successful efforts by Yasser Arafat to combat terrorism against Israel.

DEALING WITH IRAQ

U.S.-European collaboration regarding Iraq has been largely effective in recent years but is becoming increasingly strained. In 1998, some in the alliance, notably France, have seemed to wish to "normalize" Western relations with Baghdad by finding a way to lift U.N. economic sanctions, while trying to maintain some observation of Iraq's WMD capabilities. Others wonder what Washington's long-term strategy is toward Iraq, given the Clinton administration's obvious strong disinclination to use force against Iraq, until the end of 1998, as well as revelations in the media that on a half-dozen occasions the administration pressured U.N. teams not to carry out surprise inspections against suspected sensitive Iraqi sites.

And meanwhile in the region, there is as demonstrated in the recent U.S.-U.K. attack now virtually no support for the use of military action against Iraq if it stays within its borders. Finally, slow progress in the peace process and a perception, most importantly among friendly Arab regimes, that Washington is unwilling to confront what they regard as the intransigent Netanyahu government to produce greater Israeli flexibility further undermines American influence and effectiveness in the area as a whole. It appears, therefore, that Saddam Hussein is gaining and the West is losing in this long struggle over the future of Iraq's WMD capability.

What can be done about this? Preventing Iraq from building weapons of mass destruction continues to be a transatlantic vital interest in the Persian Gulf. There seems no doubt that Saddam would use a significant portion of any renewed oil resources to rekindle Iraq's WMD program as well as to begin to rebuild Iraq's conventional military capability. Neither the United States nor Europe can look favorably on Iraq's efforts to obstruct U.N. arms inspections and disregard Security Council resolutions. But the Gulf War coalition is now badly frayed and appears unable to respond effectively to these provocations. Using force against Iraq to keep Saddam in his box currently carries risks, given the weakness of the administration, the opposition of most allies, and the resistance of moderate Arab nations. Without the impetus for further joint action—including again the major use of force—in dealing with Iraq, however, the West will be left with a failing long-term strategy and Baghdad will probably possess a significant deliverable WMD capability perhaps including nuclear weapons within a decade. This would be a calamitous setback for America and its allies.

The United States and its transatlantic partners must therefore look for opportunities to reinvigorate some remnant of the Gulf War coalition and to use sustained force against Saddam Hussein, as they did in mid-December. To continue to again prevaricate endlessly on this score will only further weaken Western interests and influence in the Middle East over the long term. At the same time, U.N. Security Council sanctions must remain in place indefinitely, with a renewed and more rigorous enforcement regime to try to deny Iraq any materials that could be utilized for its WMD or ballistic missile programs. The transatlantic community also must consider further efforts to isolate Saddam and encourage his removal, even though that will not be easy. This should be a high priority.

INTERACTING WITH IRAN

The U.S. strategy of "dual containment" with respect to Iraq and Iran has failed. Iraq is slipping away from U.N. control and Iran is far from isolated, either in the region or with respect to Europe.

Indeed, Congress mistakenly passed sanctions legislation to punish the allies for not agreeing to a U.S. policy that had virtually no support anywhere in the world. At the same time, the European Union's critical dialogue with Iran produced no tangible changes in Tehran's external policies of seeking weapons of mass destruction, supporting international terrorism, and opposing the peace process.

A new transatlantic bargain therefore needs to be established to deal with an Iran that is clearly changing internally under President Khatami but whose external policies still remain a significant threat to transatlantic interests in the greater Middle East. This joint U.S.-European approach should be based on specific, agreed criteria regarding the nature over time of Tehran's international actions—especially its WMD programs—and not to Iran's domestic debates. Since it would be unrealistic to expect sharp departures over the short run in Tehran's foreign policies, an immediate distinct improvement in Iran's external behavior should not be a precondition to this fresh Western effort to improve relations with Tehran.

However, this further U.S.-European opening to Iran cannot be allowed an unlimited time to run its course, lest Iran get the benefits of interaction with the West without improving its international conduct. The United States and Europe should agree on roughly how long they will give Iran (three years?) to become a responsible regional player in the greater Middle East and, crucially, what the West should do if Iran fails the test. In the spirit of this new transatlantic accord regarding Iran, the Iran-Libya Sanctions Act should not go into effect. It would be best if it were wiped entirely from the legislative books.

Finally with respect to Iran, the allies need to become much more attentive to the dangers of Tehran's WMD programs and to the need for a transatlantic counterproliferation military capability. Although Europe has done much in recent years to improve controls on its sensitive technology transfers to the Middle East, the allies appear to believe they have therefore mostly solved the problem. To the contrary, Iran is pursuing active covert acquisition activities for its nuclear, chemical, and biological weapons programs. Europe must face up to the interrelationship between these clandestine Iranian WMD efforts and the significant additional resources that will be generated for these programs by an expansion of Iran's economic interaction with the West, especially regarding energy extraction and pipelines. If the West does not more effectively address the challenge of Iran's WMD programs, it appears likely that Tehran, like Baghdad, will possess a formidable deliverable WMD capability within a decade.

These WMD developments in both Iraq and Iran will make U.S.-European cooperation on counterproliferation increasingly important, especially with respect to theater missile defense and standoff forces.

THE CASPIAN BASIN

The Caspian basin, because of its immense energy resources, is likely in the next decade to become an area of increasing importance to the transatlantic community as a whole. At present, however, the United States appears to be dominating Western political, economic, and military interaction with the region. A more unified and strategic U.S.-European approach would lessen the appearance and reality of U.S. preeminence in the area that in turn causes special problems with Russia. It would also diversify transatlantic instruments to promote stability in the Caspian basin and—should a crisis occur there—make it more likely that the United States would have cooperative and engaged allies in trying to help manage the situation.

THE UNITED STATES, EUROPE, AND ASIA

While most Europeans are reluctant to think seriously about the traditional security implications inherent in promoting Western interests in the greater Middle East and confronting threats against them, the allies are virtually absent in Asia in this respect.

Asia, despite its current economic difficulties, will continue in the long run to be one of the most dynamic regions in the world and one of the West's greatest strategic challenges. The United States and Western Europe share vital and important interests in Asia: slowing proliferation of weapons of mass destruction; restoring Asian financial and economic stability; maintaining peace and security in the region; managing the rise of China as a regional and perhaps eventually a global power; dealing with an increasingly active India; and preventing military conflict on the Korean peninsula.

Events in Asia in the past two years have severely undermined the stability of the region and represent the following significant threats to those transatlantic interests:

—The Indian and Pakistani nuclear tests and their respective weapons and delivery systems programs;

—The Asian financial and economic crises and their domestic, regional, and global implications;

—The inability of the Japanese political system to address seriously the country's fundamental domestic ills and to provide the healthy economic growth necessary to stimulate Asian recovery;

—Renewed instability on the Korean peninsula because of North Korean nuclear and missile developments.

Except for the Asian economic crises, about which more is written in the next section of this report, the allies have been mostly uninvolved in trying to defend these Western interests and meet these threats. Despite long historic connections between Western Europe and Asia, the allies seem content to leave Asian security almost entirely in the hands of the Americans and the regional players. (Europe's multilateral engagement with Asia—the Asia-Europe meeting—has thus far been weak and ineffective.)

With respect to the nuclear tests in South Asia, European governments have been too passive, at least in public. They appear to have mostly left the management of the problem and the onus of responsibility to the Clinton administration, which has been seeking to convince India and Pakistan to refrain from mounting nuclear warheads on missiles that could deliver them; to sign the Comprehensive Test Ban Treaty; and to forgo the export of sensitive WMD and missile technologies. Apart from a small financial contribution to the Korean Economic Development Organization, Europe has done too little to promote stability on the Korean peninsula, to try to freeze and ultimately dismantle North Korea's nuclear weapons program, or to try to ensure that North Korea does not export sensitive technologies to the world's trouble spots, particularly the Middle East. This is shortsighted given the recent U.S. discovery of a suspected North Korean underground nuclear weapons facility and Pyongyang's firing of a missile over northern Japan in late August 1998. Indeed, in mid-December 1998 the 1994 U.S.-North Korea Agreed Framework is in danger of collapse, a fact that seems to have largely escaped the Europeans. The allies have also made no serious effort to persuade China to end its sensitive technology transfers to Iran and have had little to say about the P.R.C.'s nuclear and missile relationships over the years with Pakistan.

Indeed, except for the trade dimension, the allies seem disinterested in the strategic implications of the rise of Chinese power, even though China's continuing integration into the international system will have substantial consequences in the next century. Instead, Western Europe approaches China in any practical sense with an almost entirely commercial orientation. For example, it has virtually no involvement in the Taiwan issue, which is by far the most serious and immediate security question in Asia outside the Korean peninsula and the Indian subcontinent.

All this seems to be another outgrowth of Western Europe's self-preoccupation at present. Asia apparently appears a very long way away for the allies, given the many challenges Europe faces at home. The notion of Europe playing an important role in managing the balance of power and strategic equilibrium in Asia between and among Japan, China, and India seems utterly foreign on both sides of the Atlantic. This is a pity since the United States is almost entirely alone as it designs policies toward the P.R.C. and Asia more broadly, and could certainly benefit from

European involvement, assistance, and counsel. With Europe standing aside from these geopolitical challenges in Asia, the United States will be inevitably drawn toward unilateral action, some of which could seriously damage allied interests.

PRESCRIPTIONS

• The United States should maintain the clear lead in mediating negotiations between Israel and its neighbors. The EU's role should nevertheless grow over time while supporting this American effort both diplomatically and with resources to the Palestinians.

• As the negotiations between Israel and the Palestinians move into final status issues, Europeans have a right to expect that Washington confront directly and strongly either one or both of the parties when their policies are thwarting the peace process.

• The United States should increase its economic assistance to the poorer moderate Arab regimes and to the Palestinian Authority to try to address the systemic causes of societal and regime instability and to try to minimize the influence of extremist Islam in the region.

• The EU should tie its assistance to the Palestinians to a more concerted effort by the Palestinian Authority with respect to preventing terrorism against Israel.

• The United States and Europe should accelerate efforts to reinvigorate the Gulf War coalition and resume the use of sustained force against Iraq if Saddam Hussein continues to take provocative action. At the same time, the U.N. Security Council should maintain the economic sanctions on Baghdad into the foreseeable future and rigorously enforce those sanctions so as to try to deny Iraq materials that could be utilized for its WMD and ballistic missile programs.

- With respect to Iran, the United States and Europe need to forge a new strategy and opening toward Iran based on a specific set of agreed criteria regarding Tehran's external behavior.

- The allies should become much more engaged in the effort to slow Iran's acquisition of weapons of mass destruction, and Washington should share more intelligence with European governments to that end.

- The Iran-Libya Sanctions Act should be removed from the congressional books.

- Western Europe should substantially accelerate its military modernization and power projection capability to have the option of joining the United States effectively in defending Western vital interests in the greater Middle East with force, if that should become necessary. This includes intensified U.S.-European work on theater ballistic missile defenses, standoff forces, and defense industry cooperation across the Atlantic.

- A more unified and strategic U.S.-European approach to the Caspian basin is required.

- The EU and individual European governments that are now animated regarding Asia almost entirely by commercial objectives should increasingly bring the region—in particular China, Japan, the Korean peninsula, and India—into their strategic calculations and international security perspectives. This is not going to happen quickly, but given the transatlantic equities at stake in Asia, a beginning should be made.

- This will require a concerted American effort to involve the allies much more over time in developing analyses and policy options regarding Asia, including within NATO.

V. THE UNITED STATES, EUROPE, AND WORLD TRADE AND FINANCE

As this report looks to the future of Transatlantic economic, security, and diplomatic collaboration, it is telling to examine the U.S. and European reactions to the current Asian economic crises and their global impacts—the most serious financial challenge that has faced the world in a half-century. The picture that emerges is not entirely encouraging.

Both the United States and Europe were tardy in recognizing the extensive implications of the financial problems in Asia (caused by overly rigid exchange-rate systems that many Asian countries adopted, weak domestic financial systems, and the volatility of international capital markets) and were therefore slow to try to institute remedial action. Initially, Washington allowed the IMF to take the lead in handling the problem; until late December 1997, the official U.S. approach to the Asian crises was to provide policy advice to the stricken countries but not direct loans. In November 1997, President Clinton called the crises "a few glitches on the road." Only at the end of last year when it became apparent that the IMF loan program was not restoring investor confidence did the United States realize that the severity of the situation required Washington to do more.

Since then the United States has taken a vigorous role in attempting to manage the various dimensions of the economic crises in Asia. It led the effort to construct the $57 billion rescue of South Korea organized by the IMF; consistently pressed Indonesia to undertake the necessary structural reforms required by the IMF; exhorted Japan to stimulate its domestic economy and revamp its debt-ridden banking system and moribund tax code; intervened in June 1998 to stem the decline of the Japanese yen in foreign currency markets; consistently and publicly urged China not to devalue its currency; and prompted the Group of Seven (G-7) industrialized nations to the conclusion that the industrial world's chief priority at present, with the balance of risk shifting away from inflation, is to spur economic growth. And the Congress passed the administration's request for $18 billion to help replenish IMF resources (linking the additional funds to IMF reforms).

During this same period, European governments and banks have been generally supportive of these U.S. policies, including within the G-7, with respect to South Korea, Indonesia, Japan, and China. But the allies were decidedly slow to react coherently to these troublesome events in Asia, which were not initially seen in Brussels or in European national capitals as a threat to EU economies. This despite the fact that EU exports to the region are greater than those of the United States, as is the exposure of European banks through loans to the affected Asian nations. Perhaps this belated European response was caused by preoccupation with the pressing concerns of economic and monetary union and EU enlargement, a general inclination mostly to downplay events that are not occurring on or very near the continent, or an inability within the Union to agree on what to do. Recently, there are some indications that Europe might be ready to play a larger and more active role in curtailing the ongoing economic turmoil. At the fall 1998 annual IMF and World Bank meetings of finance ministers and central bankers, some European leaders even challenged American policies to date, questioning the wisdom of continued austerity programs, hinting that it might be time to consider intervening in capital markets, and suggesting ways to revamp these international financial institutions. Nevertheless, it still does not appear, at least from public documents, that Europe is shouldering an adequate share of the economic and political burden in managing these crises, which could endanger the entire global economy as well as destabilize important parts of Asia. With respect to the latter, Indonesia is a special and notably dangerous case that could blow up at any moment.

Although the Asian financial crises and their impact on the world economy are rightfully now dominating the headlines, it is important to recall in the context of this report that the U.S.-European economic relationship has been one of the great successes of the post–World War II era. The American and European economies together make up more than half of world GDP, and the United States and Europe have the largest, most stable, and most balanced trade and investment relationship in the world. Such economic interaction between the EU nations and America exceeds $1 trillion per year, and each side of the Atlantic depends deeply on the other for its economic well-being. And 95 percent of this Atlantic trade and investment takes place without difficulty or government involvement.

In December 1995, the United States and the EU sought to enlarge this transatlantic collaboration through a New Transatlantic Agenda (NTA), which is designed to increase European and global security, strengthen the multilateral trading system, build a more open trade and investment environment across the Atlantic, and address transnational challenges such as combating terrorism and protecting the environment. By all accounts, the unprecedented degree of contact and understanding among U.S. and European government officials provided by the NTA, combined with the influence and effectiveness of the Transatlantic Business Dialogue, have resulted in impressive strides so far in achieving the economic goals set forth in the NTA.

In addition, for nearly a half-century, the United States and Europe have successfully striven together to create an increasingly open environment for trade and investment throughout the world, based on the conviction that free trade is necessary not only for global prosperity but also to prevent a replay of the economic and political disasters of the 1930s. The countries of the European Union have been the most consistent and close supporters of the United States in every iteration of multilateral trade talks, beginning with the first round of the General Agreement on Tariffs and Trade (GATT) in 1947. Such sustained transatlantic economic cooperation was instrumental in establishing the World Trade Organization (WTO), is indispensable to further strengthen the WTO, and is crucial to greater liberalization of the global marketplace, including with respect to investment and financial services. And, more recently, the Asian economic crises have reminded both sides of the Atlantic of just how valuable and stable their economic relationship is.

This extraordinary record of U.S.-European cooperation does not mean that there are no economic disagreements across the

Atlantic. Washington and Brussels continue to differ on issues related to their respective tariffs and direct and indirect subsidies, particularly connected to agricultural products (bananas come to mind at present); textiles; autos, auto parts, and automotive electronics; and nonferrous metals. In addition, the two sides of the Atlantic sometimes have discordant environmental, health, safety, and regulatory standards about which they argue as well as contrasting policies on broadcasting, motion pictures, and protection of intellectual property rights for software and entertainment products. None of these bilateral trade disputes, however, threatens to knock broad U.S.-European economic interaction seriously off balance, not to say the transatlantic relationship writ large.

Besides being the largest market in trade and investment for the United States, Europe is also America's most important global competitor. The European Union has a larger volume of global trade than does the United States, and this, too, naturally upon occasion produces differences of view between Brussels and Washington. Asia has provided an especially fertile ground for U.S.-European trade competition but, again, this rivalry has been kept within acceptable boundaries and is healthy for the international economic system as a whole. Moreover, the EU is currently more supportive of U.S. trade policies than at many times in the past as the Union's positions on China's entry into the WTO and the Kodak case against Japan demonstrate.

On the other side of the ledger, a particularly contentious issue in U.S.-EU economic relations has been two pieces of extraterritorial sanctions legislation passed by Congress in recent years relating to Cuba, Iran, and Libya and directed against European individuals and companies. Despite the estimable strategic goals of these laws to promote democracy and human rights in Cuba and to address the rogue behavior of Iran and Libya, this is not an efficacious way to advance these unassailable U.S. objectives. As the above section on the greater Middle East makes clear, the United States needs its European allies in close partnership if it is to have a successful long-term policy toward that region, and particularly toward Iraq and Iran. This legislation makes such a coming together of U.S. and European policies significantly more difficult.

Put altogether, this record of transatlantic regional and global concerted action concerning trade and investment is impressive and, on balance with occasional ups and downs, it is likely to continue. The next transatlantic step is to open further trade and investment between the United States and Europe.

PRESCRIPTIONS

• The EU and allied governments should play a more active private and more visible public part in attempting to manage with the United States the regional and global implications of the Asian economic crises.

• Such an increased and prominent role for Europe will be possible only if Washington is willing to engage in more intense coordination with the other side of the Atlantic regarding U.S. deliberations on how best to deal with the myriad global challenges triggered by Asia's economic turmoil.

• With the United States and Europe out front, the G-7 should urgently examine ways to reform the global financial architecture to better predict and deal with future crises.

• Led by recent actions by the United States, the G-7 should informally seek to coordinate with their central banks a round of interest rate reductions by the industrial democracies.

• Transatlantic nations should continue to press Japan vigorously to restart its economy, implement its commitment to banking reform, stimulate consumer demand, deregulate key economic sectors, and open its markets to fair trade. This would help stop a further deterioration in the Asian and global economies.

• Congress should support U.S. contributions to the IMF and at the same time continue to press for fundamental IMF reforms.

- Congress should urgently pass fast-track legislation to give the president enhanced authority to negotiate international trade agreements.

- The United States and the European Union should become more ambitious by beginning to negotiate step by step a genuinely open trade and investment area—a true single transatlantic market—with real deadlines.

- Washington and Brussels should continue to push hard for multilateral liberalization within the WTO, including in the agricultural talks beginning in 1999 and the services negotiations in 2000.

- Both sides of the Atlantic should guard vigorously against protectionist pressures, especially in the new, more difficult global economic environment; the United States and Europe should want more competition based on fair rules of the road/level playing field, not less.

- The U.S. Congress should remove from the legislation books as soon as possible the Cuban Liberation and Democratic Solidarity Act and, as prescribed earlier, the Iran-Libya Sanctions Act.

VI. NEW THREATS TO TRANSATLANTIC INTERESTS

Transnational challenges, which range from the proliferation of weapons of mass destruction as discussed in this report to terrorism to environmental problems to crime and drugs have been receiving more transatlantic attention in the past decade. Because these new threats cross territorial borders, they also blur the line between domestic and foreign policies.

The spread of weapons of mass destruction is likely to be an ever more serious problem for the West during the next decade. International terrorism is back in the news and higher on the U.S.-

European agenda after the attacks on U.S. embassies in Kenya and Tanzania; it would be surprising if these are the last such attacks on American facilities and citizens abroad. Cyberterrorism probably also has a real future in our increasingly interdependent and democratic societies. Environmental degradation is a rising preoccupation among governments and ordinary people on both sides of the Atlantic, particularly regarding the issue of global warming as demonstrated during the December 1997 Conference on Climate Change held in Kyoto, Japan. One can expect more and more problems for the transatlantic community as well from international organized crime, narcotics trafficking, and migration and refugee flows. Finally, greater international travel makes the United States and Europe more vulnerable than before to the spread of infectious diseases.

PRESCRIPTIONS

• The proliferation of weapons of mass destruction, international terrorism, environmental degradation, organized crime and narcotics trafficking, destabilizing migration, and the spread of infectious diseases all represent new challenges during the next decade for the U.S.-European relationship. Some progress has been made but there are still important consultative, analytical, and policy gaps to be filled, most urgently concerning WMD proliferation and global warming. Both these issues need to be much higher on the transatlantic agenda than heretofore.

VII. CONCLUSION

The United States and Europe are the only conceivable global partners for each other in seeking to shape the international system in positive ways into the next century.

Without America, Europe will tend to retreat into a continental fortress mentality or into sustained passivity as threats from beyond the continent progressively build and then intrude into the interests and daily lives of the allies.

Without Europe, the United States will likely alternate between brief and usually ineffective spasms of unilateralism interspersed with occasional temptations to withdraw substantially from messy international life.

A growing transatlantic partnership consistent with the regional and global challenges of the next century will increasingly protect the vital and important interests of both the United States and Europe, and thus the basic welfare of their citizens.

As Henry Kissinger has put it, "On both sides of the Atlantic, the next phase of our foreign policy will require restoration of some of the dedication, attitudes and convictions of common destiny that brought us to this point—though, of course, under totally new conditions."

This will entail deliberate and sustained statesmanship as well as innumerable acts of detailed and coordinated policy implementation on the part of Europe and the United States over many years. There is no time to waste.

ADDITIONAL VIEWS

I endorse the broad thrust of the report but append the following additional view. This report properly concludes that strong transatlantic ties remain a vital mutual interest and contains excellent prescriptions. It has, however, one important failing. While updating specific issues from the Cold War's end, it focuses anachronistically on security's political-military aspects and gives inadequate weight to interdependent political-economic aspects. Its thrust is that with NATO's relevance reaffirmed, security questions in Europe have been answered, and it is time for Europeans to step up to "out of area" military challenges where the United States shoulders a disproportionate burden. In fact, the great European strategic issue remains open. The report acknowledges allied preoccupation with making the European Union a larger, more effective global actor, but it implies this is relatively marginal, if not diversionary, from the age's main requirements. However, the EU agenda for Europe's political integration—common currency, internal reform, enlargement, common foreign policy—is *the* historic challenge of the new millennium's first decade. In an era fortunately lacking world-class threats to U.S. military dominance but increasingly requiring political, economic, and financial muscle to solve problems that affect every nation's stability, it has great security importance to Americans. How well the EU succeeds will determine whether Europe is stable and whether the United States acquires a global partner to address increasingly significant nonmilitary threats to common security. I regret the missed opportunity to educate citizens about a poorly understood institution and the stakes in its endeavor to create preconditions for a modern security partnership—including how problematic what the United States desires for NATO will be if the EU fails. Too little is thus done to stimulate reflection on the difficult changes required in America's approach to transatlantic relations if we find ourselves soon with a partner that has strength and standing to demand genuinely equal, not junior status.

G. Jonathan Greenwald

I endorse the broad thrust of the report, but append the following additional view. A key recommendation of the report is that it is in American self-interest that Europe play a greater role in global affairs. In the past, because a united Europe ensured a strong American ally, the United States vigorously supported Europe's efforts to form the European Community, to create a single internal market, and to launch the Euro. But European preoccupation with these tasks has inhibited European engagement in the Middle East, Asia, and other regions of the world where the United States and Europe have common interests. In the future, before the United States supports an even larger European Union and bigger NATO, it should weigh the benefits of that expansion against the costs of having a Europe that continues to be self-absorbed and thus unable to more fully share the burden of world leadership. In theory, a more tightly knit Europe will be a stronger one, better able to be America's partner in the world. That has always been the implicit bargain Washington has made with Brussels. But that deal breaks down if European unification is open-ended and, as a result, in any relevant time frame, Europe will never be quite ready to be America's global partner.

Bruce Stokes

I endorse the broad thrust of the report but append the following additional view. The financial crises that have engulfed many emerging countries in Asia, Latin America, and Eastern Europe show that the International Monetary Fund is not adequate for the challenges of the next century. To carry out its stabilizing role, the fund must acquire more of the characteristics of a world central bank. It must create the incentives for genuine financial surveillance and transparent accounting by banks and large corporations throughout the world, and it must publicly assess the ability of national central banks to adhere to their exchange-rate regimes and inflation targets. Finally, it must have the resources to act as lender of last resort for those countries and banks that have maintained prudent financial practices and policies.

The only way a new, meaner, and well-financed fund can emerge is through cooperation between the United States and Europe. Prime Minister Blair has issued the call. The leaders of Europe and the United States should now respond.

Gary Hufbauer

I share the thrust of this thoughtful and honest report—that America and Europe have an opportunity to build on shared interests to move toward a more global, and more real, partnership. That goal will not be achieved today or tomorrow, but it is the right goal. However, the report somewhat overstates, I believe, the Russian and loose-nukes predicament for transatlantic policy. Russia surely shares the U.S. and European stake in not seeing its nuclear wherewithal spread into its neighborhood. If Russia fell into chaos or civil war, which does not seem likely, that would be a real danger. It is not, however, one the United States and its partners can do much about. The partners should be generous with Russia, but government assistance is not going to rebuild Russia; only Russian policies that make the country attractive for private investment can do that. So far, the record of helping Russia is perhaps the worst of all worlds: what the transatlantic partners have done is enough to convince their publics, especially in the United States, that Russia is a bottomless, futile pit, while Russians rightly regard the response from abroad as niggardly.

Gregory F. Treverton

Although I endorse the broad thrust of the report, this otherwise excellent document deals with U.S.-West European rather than U.S.-European relations. It thus misses the transformation of Europe since the end of the Cold War.

Charles Gati

DISSENTING VIEWS

We endorse the broad thrust of the report but append this dissenting view regarding the specific assertions and recommendations concerning NATO enlargement.

NATO enlargement must be a process driven by the interests of the alliance, taking into account the ability of those European democracies aspiring for membership to make a net contribution to the security and capabilities of the alliance. NATO's decision to extend membership only to Poland, Hungary, and the Czech Republic at this time recognizes that not all new applicants are equally ready to be security allies. Some may never be. But at the same time, NATO must not prejudge Europe's future by imposing any arbitrary time lines. To do so would contradict the very essence of Article 10 of the North Atlantic Treaty and the alliance's open-door policy as enshrined in the Madrid Declaration.

Thus, the three- to five-year artificial pause in the NATO enlargement process prescribed in the report would be a mistake, raising again the specter of a Europe divided. The U.S. Senate, in its ratification debate on enlargement, recognized this danger and therefore rejected such a pause, lest its actions precipitate a destabilizing backlash or a loss of momentum in the reform processes of NATO aspirants and neighbors. Although we must not allow NATO to collapse under its own weight, insinuating that the accession of additional members would turn the alliance into a debating club is misleading. Furthermore, the alliance must not cede its freedom (formally or informally) to make a determination on future members at the appropriate time out of concern for Russia's possible reaction. For all these reasons, the assertions and recommendations in the report regarding NATO enlargement would certainly not serve the transatlantic interest in expanding the zone of peace and stability throughout post–Cold War Europe.

Ian J. Brzezinski
Paula J. Dobriansky
Charles Gati
Michael H. Haltzel
Bruce Pitcairn Jackson
F. Stephen Larrabee
Kenneth A. Myers III
Simon Serfaty
Helmut Sonnenfeldt
Marc A. Thiessen
Gregory F. Treverton

Although we endorse the broad thrust of the report, we disagree with the statement that today's U.S. Congress is "less attentive to foreign affairs than any since the 1930s." Congress is far more informed and engaged in foreign affairs than it used to be. This is due to many geopolitical and domestic factors, but above all it is due to the information age. Today, Congress is deluged with information and perspectives on world affairs. The result has been not ignorance but debate and dissent. Developing consensus in Congress consequently may be a greater challenge, but the degree of difficulty has lately been escalated more by a lack of confidence in the executive branch than by the absence of knowledge.

Ian J. Brzezinski
Marc A. Thiessen

Although I endorse the broad thrust of the report, the prescriptions regarding the Israeli-Palestinian peace process do not confront the divisive challenge that this issue seems certain to pose for the allies during the coming year.

By the Oslo Accords, Israel and the PLO agreed that the permanent status of the occupied territories (covering borders, settlements, security, refugees, and Jerusalem) would be based on the implementation of Security Council Resolution 242 and begin no later than May 4, 1999. Resolution 242 calls for "Israeli withdrawal from occupied territories" and mutual recognition and respect for territorial integrity and security within recognized borders.

Netanyahu and his Likud regime clearly have no intention of complying with the Oslo commitments or Resolution 242. To provide a pretext, Netanyahu demands impossible perfection in preventing violence (consider Rabin's murder and Goldberg's massacre), meanwhile stalling the transitional withdrawals, expanding settlements, and taking other provocative actions. In general, he has defied the United States, which has proved to be a paper tiger. His government's intentions for the permanent status are indicated by naming Ariel Sharon (an extreme hawk) as permanent status negotiator and by several draft maps, which show Israel annexing over half of the West Bank (including some 140 of the illegal settlements) and leaving the Palestinians with two or three separate, noncontiguous areas, plus Gaza. These areas would be wholly surrounded by the Israeli-annexed territory and crisscrossed by Israeli highways serving the Israeli settlements. The Palestinian regime, in effect, would remain at the mercy of Israeli coercion and control, and could not become a viable independent state.

This outcome would make a mockery of Oslo and 242 and be a formula not for a "just and lasting peace" seeking "historic reconciliation," as Rabin and Arafat had hoped, but for continued conflict, terror, and repression (consider Hebron). It would ratify, not reverse, past Israeli illegalities. The Palestinian Authority will surely reject such a permanent status and might precipitate a major crisis by proclaiming a Palestinian state on May 4, 1999. Only forceful pressure on Israel will offer any hope for a constructive outcome. If, for the reasons discussed in the report, the United States does not provide such leadership, the European Union, which has substantial leverage through its trade with Israel, should chart its own course for achieving a just and durable peace.

Robert R. Bowie

If the thrust of the report is transatlantic solidarity, I strongly concur. But I have some concerns.

The report probably understates the challenge. With the Soviet collapse, a Gaullist theme is heard in Europe (and elsewhere) that American dominance is one of the world's major problems and that counterweights are needed. Many U.S.-European disagreements are thus not merely "tactical," as the report says, but structural. Indeed, as European defense spending shrinks, Europe will become all the more dependent on the United States in the security realm even as it asserts a new economic and foreign policy independence—further complicating relations.

On specifics, I have to reject the "pause" in NATO enlargement. NATO should deliberate on this at whatever pace is natural. A fixed hiatus is gratuitous, tendentious, and probably destabilizing.

There is a certain escapism about the security of some aspirant countries. The clear implication is that the Balts, for example, are excluded because of Russia's reaction—as if the Molotov-Ribbentrop pact were our guiding policy. NATO cannot possibly tolerate a new Russian domination of the Balts, on any pretext, whatever the best formula for deterring this. Similarly Ukraine.

The Russia problem, in general, is understated. Whatever Russia's internal weakness, its increasingly nationalist foreign policy (weapons to Iran and China; bullying Latvia) should warrant some consideration as the West ruminates on further bailouts.

The Mideast discussion is clichéd. U.S. policy is criticized for not "confronting" Netanyahu enough. This misunderstands the real problem. Netanyahu has been telling us for two years that the incrementalism of Oslo (designed for a Labor government) is a nightmare for him, and a different procedure (i.e., moving directly to final status) would have made flexibility easier. The United States has mishandled this, but not in the manner suggested.

On Turkey, I fear that a relaxation of U.S. badgering of the EU would only perpetuate the EU's strategic shortsightedness.

Peter W. Rodman

I endorse the broad thrust of the report but append the following dissenting view. This report contains much excellent analysis and many prescriptions with which I concur. With others, however, I differ. For example, NATO must be clear-sighted in what it does next on enlargement, especially to ensure that its strength is in no way compromised. Yet I believe that the commitment represented by NATO's "open door" policy does not permit the mandating of a pause, formal or informal, in further invitations to join. Nor do I believe NATO should defer to Russia in deciding on the pace or direction of enlargement—as important as it is to help Russia succeed internally and play a positive role in European security. Indeed, the report should be even more forthcoming about Western support for Russian economic recovery. Further afield, on Arab-Israeli peacemaking, I do not accept the conclusion that Europeans can expect Washington to "confront directly and strongly" either party, "when their policies are thwarting the peace process." My experience has been that building confidence, not confrontation—especially with Israel—better sustains the peace process. Also, while I would welcome greater European involvement in the "Greater Middle East," I believe that making this a necessary task for NATO would likely undercut its role closer to home. In general, I take a more positive view than much of the report about the current state of transatlantic relations, and thus I am also more optimistic about their future.

Robert E. Hunter

Although I endorse the broad thrust of the report, I disagree with the prescription that "The Iran-Libya Sanctions Act should be removed from the Congressional books." The Iran-Libya Sanctions Act of 1996 (ILSA) has been extremely effective in deterring many U.S. and non-U.S. companies from making significant investments in Iranian and Libyan oil and gas projects. Multinationals have been hesitant in responding to Iran's 1995 international tender of 11 large projects, primarily owing—as Iranian officials themselves concede—to the economic and political uncertainty generated by ILSA and other U.S. sanctions targeted against Iran. Libya similarly has had no success in attracting significant investments.

Even last year's $2 billion agreement of the Total/Gazprom/Petronas consortium to develop the South Pars oil field off the coast of Iran must be seen as an anomaly. Earlier this year, the State Department waived sanctions against these investors or other non-U.S. companies that might invest in Iran in the future. Yet, no other major investments in Iran have occurred since the waiver was announced. An earlier agreement to develop South Pars was signed in 1993, but the project never moved forward.

Of course, the extraterritorial aspect of ILSA has prompted severe criticism from European and Asian governments and businesses. Nevertheless, it is occasionally necessary for the U.S. government to finesse the rules of international law when matters of fundamental foreign policy interest are at stake. In November 1995, former Undersecretary of State Peter Tarnoff stated, "A straight line links Iran's oil income and its ability to sponsor terrorism, build weapons of mass destruction, and acquire sophisticated armaments." Thus, it would be irresponsible to invoke principles of extraterritoriality and international comity as reasons for not taking effective steps to block these projects or make them more expensive. ILSA also gives the U.S. government more leverage (i.e., an offer to withdraw the threat of ILSA sanctions) in direct negotiations with Iran and Libya, should those countries choose to moderate their behavior.

Fred W. Reinke

Because the report makes many good recommendations (e.g., working to ensure Turkey's Western orientation, maintaining sanctions and being prepared to use force against Iraq, supporting Ukraine's independence and territorial integrity, strong action in Kosovo, calling on our European allies to accelerate their military modernization, etc.), I do not dissent from the overall report. However, I have many serious differences with a number of the report's other conclusions, particularly those concerning NATO expansion (which are discussed above in more detail).

Further, I strongly disagree with the recommendation for "giving more substance" to the NATO-Russia Permanent Joint Council (PJC). To the contrary, NATO must be vigilant in ensuring that the PJC remains nothing more than a forum for explaining—not negotiating—NATO policy with Russia. Russia must be given neither a voice nor a veto in NATO decision-making. And while NATO must indeed be prepared to meet the new security challenges of the next century, the way to ensure this is to make certain that NATO's strategic concept and military planning remain firmly focused on territorial defense.

I also strongly disagree with the report's recommendation that the United States continue pouring good money after bad into the dysfunctional IMF. With its bailouts, the IMF encourages risky, unwise investments that would not otherwise be made, and then imposes destructive high-tax and antigrowth policies on recipient countries, ensuring they cannot grow out of their debt. The IMF should be radically overhauled or abolished.

Most important, however, I object to the prescriptions related to Helms-Burton and ILSA. With the recent admission by the European Union (in the proposed U.S.-EU agreement) that their nationals have indeed been trafficking in stolen American property in Cuba, and the acknowledgment that adjustments are needed in international law to deter such illegal activity, the Helms-Burton law has been vindicated. For all the huffing and puffing and threats of recrimination, the European Union has conceded the basic principle of Helms-Burton: that trafficking in stolen property is wrong. Now, having admitted to the crime, our European friends are left only to complain about the punishment.

And even in those complaints, they are mistaken. The law is not extraterritorial, as the EU contends. It affects only those who traffic in stolen American property in Cuba—as long as they steer clear of such properties, Europeans are free to do business with Castro. And the penalties—denial of entry into the United States, judgments against their property in the United States—are not extraterritorial either. The United States has a right and an obligation to take actions within its borders to protect the property rights of its nationals. Until the EU is prepared to enforce ironclad measures against illegal trafficking, Congress is unlikely to enact any changes in the Helms-Burton law, much less repeal it.

The fact is that the Helms-Burton law works, despite its tepid enforcement by the Clinton administration. The STETT-ITT deal—in which a European trafficker was forced to compensate the legitimate American owners for the use of their property in Cuba—would never have happened without Helms-Burton. The law has discouraged investment in stolen properties in Cuba, denying Castro the use of these stolen properties to finance his machinery of internal oppression. Thus, the law has also helped increase the isolation of the Castro regime—an isolation that certainly played a role in Castro's decision to invite the Pope to Cuba.

The sad fact remains that, faced with double-digit unemployment, enormous government regulation, and anemic economies struggling under statist fiscal policies, many European governments have begun to employ increasingly mercantilist foreign policies. The United States, by contrast, places moral (and security) considerations higher on its foreign policy agenda. This is the underlying cause of the tension between the United States and the EU over both Helms-Burton and the Iran-Libya Sanctions Act. These laws have simply exposed a fault line that separates the United States and Europe, and these differences will continue to be an issue of contention in the transatlantic relationship.

Marc A. Thiessen

MEMBERS OF THE TASK FORCE

Members of the Independent Task Force were invited to endorse the general policy thrust and prescriptions in this report, although not all members necessarily subscribe fully to every finding and recommendation. Members who submitted additional or dissenting views are indicated below.

ROBERT D. BLACKWILL, Adjunct Senior Fellow at the Council on Foreign Relations, is the Belfer Lecturer in International Security at Harvard University's John F. Kennedy School of Government. He is also Faculty Chair of the School's Executive Programs for U.S. and Russian General Officers and for members of the Russian State Duma; of the Kennedy School's Initiative on U.S.-China Relations; and of the Executive Program for Senior Chinese Military Officers. His last position in government was as President George Bush's Special Assistant for Soviet and European Affairs.

ROBERT R. BOWIE[†] is Dillon Professor of International Affairs, Emeritus, at Harvard University. He previously served as Deputy Director for Intelligence at the Central Intelligence Agency, and Director of the Harvard Center for International Affairs.

CHARLES G. BOYD, a retired General in the U.S. Air Force, is Executive Director of the National Security Study Group.

IAN J. BRZEZINSKI[†] is Legislative Assistant for National Security Affairs in the Office of Senator William K. Roth Jr. (R-Del.). He assists Senator Roth on foreign policy and national defense matters, including the coordination of the Senate NATO Observer Group.

Note: Institutional affiliations are for identification purposes only.
*Individual endorses the broad thrust of the report but appends an additional view.
[†]Individual endorses the broad thrust of the report but appends a dissenting view.

CAMILLE M. CAESAR is an associate attorney in transactional practice at Kirkland & Ellis.

REBA CARRUTH is Assistant Professor and Director of the Transatlantic (NAFTA/EU) Project at the George Washington University. She is a former Regional Market Analyst for Honeywell Europe S.A. in Brussels.

JACQUELYN K. DAVIS is Executive Vice President of the Institute for Foreign Policy Analysis and President of National Security Planning Associates. She previously served as Chairperson of the Defense Advisory Committee on Women in the Services.

PAULA J. DOBRIANSKY† is Vice President and Washington Director of the Council on Foreign Relations. She is also the Council's first George F. Kennan Senior Fellow for Russian and Eurasian Studies. During the Reagan administration, she served as Director of European and Soviet Affairs at the National Security Council.

SAM FEIST is the Senior Producer of CNN's Washington-based public affairs programs *Late Edition with Wolf Blitzer* and *Evans, Novak, Hunt and Shields.*

ELLEN L. FROST is a Visiting Fellow at the Institute for International Economics. She previously served as Counselor to the U.S. Trade Representative and to the Deputy Assistant Secretary of Defense.

ALTON FRYE is the Presidential Senior Fellow at the Council on Foreign Relations. A former Council president, he now directs the Council's Program on Congress and U.S. Foreign Policy.

CHARLES GATI*† is Senior Vice President of Interinvest. He is also a Fellow at the Foreign Policy Institute of the Paul H. Nitze School of Advanced International Studies, Johns Hopkins University.

Members of the Task Force

TOBY T. GATI is a Senior International Adviser at Akin, Gump, Strauss, Hauer & Feld, L.L.P. She previously served as Special Assistant to the President and Senior Director for Russia, Ukraine and the Eurasian States at the National Security Council at the beginning of the Clinton administration and then as Assistant Secretary of State for Intelligence and Research.

DAVID C. GOMPERT is Vice President of the RAND Corporation. He was Special Assistant to President George Bush and to Secretary of State Henry Kissinger.

G. JONATHAN GREENWALD* is Scarff Distinguished Visiting Professor of Diplomacy and Foreign Policy at Lawrence University. He previously served as Minister-Counselor at the U.S. Mission to the European Union.

MICHAEL H. HALTZEL† is Minority Staff Director of the Subcommittee on European Affairs, U.S. Senate Committee on Foreign Relations. He was Chief of the European Division at the Library of Congress and Director of West European Studies at the Woodrow Wilson Center.

F. WILLIAM HAWLEY is Chairman of CSI Research and Education Foundation. He is a former Director of International Government Relations at Citicorp/Citibank and Assistant Director of the Council on International Economic Policy in the White House.

GARY HUFBAUER* is Reginald Jones Senior Fellow at the Institute for International Economics. He has been Director of Studies at the Council on Foreign Relations, a professor at Georgetown University, and Deputy Assistant Secretary at the U.S. Department of the Treasury.

Note: Institutional affiliations are for identification purposes only.
*Individual endorses the broad thrust of the report but appends an additional view.
†Individual endorses the broad thrust of the report but appends a dissenting view.

ROBERT E. HUNTER† is Senior Adviser at the RAND Corporation and serves on the Pentagon's Defense Policy Board. He previously served as U.S. Ambassador to NATO.

BRUCE PITCAIRN JACKSON† is President and cofounder of the U.S. Committee on NATO. He previously served in the U.S. Department of Defense.

KENNETH I. JUSTER is a Senior Partner at the law firm of Arnold & Porter, where he practices international law. He previously served as the Counselor (Acting) of the U.S. Department of State and Senior Adviser to the Deputy U.S. Secretary of State.

CRAIG KENNEDY is President of the German Marshall Fund of the United States.

KAY KING is Executive Director of the Association of Professional Schools of International Affairs (APSIA). She is a former legislative aide to Senator Joseph R. Biden Jr. (D-Del.).

F. STEPHEN LARRABEE† is a Senior Consultant at the RAND Corporation.

JAMES G. LOWENSTEIN is a Senior Consultant at APCO Associates. He formerly served as U.S. Ambassador to Luxembourg, Principal Deputy Assistant Secretary of State for European Affairs, and a member of staff of the U.S. Senate Committee on Foreign Relations.

CHRISTOPHER MAKINS is a Senior Adviser to the German Marshall Fund of the United States. He is a former Executive Vice President, Policy Programs, at the Aspen Institute.

MARTIN MCCUSKER is a Senior Consultant at DFI International in Washington, D.C. He previously served as Director of the Defense and Security Committee in the NATO Parliamentary Assembly in Brussels and Deputy Director of East-West Studies at the Aspen Institute.

Members of the Task Force

ERIC D.K. MELBY is a Senior Fellow at the Forum for International Policy. He previously served on the National Security Council staff, the U.S. Department of State, USAID, the International Energy Agency, and the Peace Corps.

KENNETH A. MYERS III† is a Legislative Assistant for Foreign Affairs and National Security to Senator Richard G. Lugar (R-Ind.).

EARL C. RAVENAL is Distinguished Senior Fellow of the Cato Institute and Professor Emeritus at Georgetown University School of Foreign Service. He is a former official in the Office of the Secretary of Defense.

FRED W. REINKE† is of counsel at the law firm of Milbank, Tweed, Hadley & McCloy, specializing in international trade and regulatory matters and complex commercial and international litigation.

DONALD H. RIVKIN is Senior Counsel at Schnader, Harrison, Segal & Lewis, LLP. He is a former Director of the British-American Chamber of Commerce and Chair of the American Bar Association.

PETER W. RODMAN† is Director of National Security Programs at the Nixon Center for Peace and Freedom. He previously served as Deputy Assistant to the President for National Security Affairs and as Director of the U.S. Department of State's Policy Planning Staff.

GEBHARD SCHWEIGLER is a Senior Research Associate at Stiftung Wissenschaft und Politik, in Germany. He has been a visiting professor at Georgetown University and Dartmouth College, and an Associate at the Carnegie Endowment for International Peace.

Note: Institutional affiliations are for identification purposes only.
*Individual endorses the broad thrust of the report but appends an additional view.
†Individual endorses the broad thrust of the report but appends a dissenting view.

SIMON SERFATY[†] is Professor of U.S. Foreign Policy with the Graduate Programs in International Studies at Old Dominion University, and Senior Associate and Director of European Studies at the Center for Strategic and International Studies.

HELMUT SONNENFELDT[†] is a Guest Scholar at the Brookings Institution. He is a former senior staff member at the National Security Council, Counselor to the U.S. Department of State, and Director of the Atlantic Council of the United States.

ANGELA STENT, Professor of Government at Georgetown University, serves on the boards of the U.S.-Russia Business Forum and Women in International Security.

BRUCE STOKES[*] is a Senior Fellow at the Council on Foreign Relations. He directs the Council's project on U.S.-European economic relations in the 21st century.

MARC THIESSEN[†] is Press Spokesman for the U.S. Senate Committee on Foreign Relations.

GREGORY F. TREVERTON[*†] is Vice President of the Pacific Council on International Policy.

MARSHA VANDEBERG is the author and editor of the on-line VandeBerg World Report (which can be found through the Electric Library at www.elibrary.com), providing coverage and analysis of major international events and individuals.

Note: Institutional affiliations are for identification purposes only.
[*]Individual endorses the broad thrust of the report but appends an additional view.
[†]Individual endorses the broad thrust of the report but appends a dissenting view.

OBSERVERS

Observers participated in Task Force discussions but, because of their official capacities, were not asked to sign on to the report's conclusions.

PHILIP BOBBITT is Senior Director for Critical Infrastructure on the National Security Council staff. He previously served as Director for Intelligence at the National Security Council.

JÜRGEN CHROBOG is Ambassador of Germany to the United States. He is a former Political Director, and Spokesman, for the German Foreign Ministry, and was an adviser to Foreign Minsters Hans-Dietrich Genscher and Klaus Kinkel.

BRUCE CLARK is International Security Editor at *The Economist*.

JONATHAN DAVIDSON is Head of Academic Affairs and Foreign Policy Adviser at the Delegation of the European Commission in Washington, D.C. He is a former Director of the University of South Carolina's Washington office and a member of the British Diplomatic Service.

JOY DRUCKER is a Legislative Assistant for Foreign Affairs in the Office of the House Democratic Leader.

MARSHA A. ECHOLS is a Professor at Howard University Law School, where she teaches international business transactions, international economic law, and international technology transfer.

Note: Institutional affiliations are for identification purposes only.

DANIEL HAMILTON is Associate Director of the Policy Planning Staff at the U.S. Department of State. He is a former Policy Adviser to the Assistant Secretary for European Affairs and Ambassador to Germany, and was a Senior Associate at the Carnegie Endowment for International Peace.

JIM HOAGLAND, Associate Editor and Chief Foreign Correspondent of the *Washington Post*, writes a column on international affairs that appears twice weekly in the *Post* and is internationally syndicated.

FRANK G. KLOTZ, a Colonel in the U.S. Air Force, was a 1997–98 Military Fellow at the Council on Foreign Relations.

CHARLES KUPCHAN is a Senior Fellow at the Council on Foreign Relations and a Professor of International Relations at Georgetown University. He served on the National Security Council staff during the first Clinton administration.

BARRY LOWENKRON is National Intelligence Officer for Europe at the National Intelligence Council. He previously served as Director of European Affairs at the National Security Council and Special Assistant to the Chairman of the Joint Chiefs of Staff.

SVEND B. MADSEN is Minister and Deputy Chief of Mission at the Embassy of Denmark to the United States. He is a former head of the U.S. Department in Denmark's Ministry of Foreign Affairs.

THOMAS MATUSSEK is Minister and Deputy Chief of Mission at the Embassy of Germany to the United States. He was Head of Office and Chief of Staff, respectively, under German Foreign Ministers Hans-Dietrich Genscher and Klaus Kinkel.

LARS MOLLER is a Minister (Economics) at the Embassy of Denmark to the United States. He previously worked in Denmark's Ministry of Foreign Affairs.

Observers

HUGO PAEMEN is Ambassador and Head of the Delegation of the European Commission to the United States. He previously served in senior positions in the European Commission and in Belgium's embassies in Geneva, Paris, and Washington, D.C.

BARRY PAVEL is Acting Principal Director of Strategy in the Office of the U.S. Secretary of Defense, where he contributes to the development and review of defense policy and strategy documents.

JOHN B. RICHARDSON is Deputy Head of Mission for the Delegation of the European Commission to the United States.

FERDINANDO SALLEO is Ambassador of Italy to the United States. He previously served as Italy's Ambassador to the Soviet Union and to the Organization for Economic Cooperation and Development (OECD), and was Development, Economic, and Political Director and Secretary General in the Italian Ministry of Foreign Affairs.

JOHN SAWERS is a Counsellor, dealing with foreign and defense policy, at the Embassy of the United Kingdom to the United States. A former fellow at Harvard University's Center for International Affairs, he served as Chief of Staff to British Foreign Secretary Douglas Hurd.

VOLKER SCHLEGEL is Minister (Economics) at the Embassy of Germany to the United States. He previously served in the German Embassy to Iran and the Foreign Ministry, as well as private-sector positions in law and business.

JOHN F. SOPKO, Chief Counsel for Special Matters at the U.S. Department of Commerce, advises the Secretary and other senior officials on sensitive legal issues. He advised Senator Sam Nunn (D-Ga.) on national security and criminal justice issues.

Note: Institutional affiliations are for identification purposes only.

STEFANO STEFANINI is Senior Political Counselor at the Embassy of Italy to the United States, dealing with political and military affairs. He follows U.S. foreign policy and specializes in the Balkans, European security, NATO, and U.S.-Russian relations.

PAMELA THIESSEN serves as Senator Rod Grams's (R-Minn.) staff representative to the U.S. Senate Committee on Foreign Relations, where he is Chairman of the Subcommittee on International Operations.

K.E. TYGESEN is Ambassador of Denmark to the United States. He is a former Ambassador to Germany and Brazil, and was Denmark's State Secretary for European and Foreign Economic Affairs.

E. ANTHONY WAYNE is Principal Deputy Assistant Secretary of State for European and Canadian Affairs at the U.S. Department of State.

ANNE WITKOWSKY is Director for Defense Policy and Arms Control on the National Security Council staff. She served in the office of the Secretary of Defense from 1988 to 1993.

STEPHEN WRIGHT is Minister at the Embassy of the United Kingdom to the United States.

Note: Institutional affiliations are for identification purposes only.

DISCUSSION SESSIONS AND PRESENTERS
SEPTEMBER 1997–APRIL 1998

September 1997

How Much Does the Transatlantic Relationship Matter After the End of the Cold War?

JÜRGEN CHROBOG, Ambassador of the Federal Republic of Germany to the United States, German Embassy

DAVID C. GOMPERT, Vice President, RAND

EARL C. RAVENAL, Distinguished Senior Fellow, Cato Institute

October 1997

The Domestic Contexts of the Transatlantic Relationship

BRUCE CLARK, Washington Correspondent, *Financial Times*

THOMAS E. MANN, Director, Governmental Studies, The Brookings Institution

GEBHARD SCHWEIGLER, Senior Research Associate, Stiftung Wissenschaft und Politik

November 1997

The Implications of the EU Economic and Monetary Union for Transatlantic Relations

WALTER RUSSELL MEAD, President's Fellow, World Policy Institute, New School for Social Research

The Future of Transatlantic Relations

JOHN B. RICHARDSON, Deputy Head of Mission, Delegation of the European Commission to the United States

December 1997

U.S.-European Economic Relations and World Trade

ELLEN L. FROST, Senior Fellow, Institute for International Economics

HUGO PAEMEN, Head of Mission, Delegation of the European Commission to the United States

MARC THIESSEN, Press Spokesman, U.S. Senate Committee on Foreign Relations

January 1998

The United States, Europe, and the Greater Middle East

RICHARD FALKENRATH, Executive Director, Belfer Center for Science and International Affairs, John F. Kennedy School of Government, Harvard University

PETER RODMAN, Director of National Security Programs, The Nixon Center

JOHN SAWERS, Counsellor, British Embassy

February 1998

The United States, Europe, and Asia

PAULINE GREEN, Member of the European Parliament

ROBERT KAGAN, Senior Associate, The Carnegie Endowment for International Peace

[78]

DAVID M. LAMPTON, George and Sadie Hyman Professor of China Studies and Director of China Studies, School of Advanced International Studies, The Johns Hopkins University

WERNER SCHÜLE, Counselor for Economic and Financial Affairs, Delegation of the European Commission to the United States

March 1998

The United States, Europe, and the New Security Threats

JAMES W. CICCONI, Partner, Akin, Gump, Strauss, Hauer & Feld, L.L.P.

JOHN F. SOPKO, Chief Counsel for Special Matters, Office of the General Counsel, United States Department of Commerce

STEFANO STEFANINI, Senior Political Counselor, Italian Embassy

KONRAD VON MOLTKE, Adjunct Professor and Senior Fellow, Institute on International Environmental Governance, Dartmouth College

April 1998

The United States, Europe, Russia, and European Security

ARNOLD HORELICK, Vice President for Russian and Eurasian Affairs, The Carnegie Endowment for International Peace

KARL KAISER, Otto Wolff Director, Research Institute of the German Society for Foreign Affairs

DIMITRI K. SIMES, President, The Nixon Center

WILLIAM WALLACE, Reader in International Relations, London School of Economics

OTHER REPORTS OF INDEPENDENT TASK FORCES SPONSORED BY THE COUNCIL ON FOREIGN RELATIONS

* †*After the Tests: U.S. Policy Toward India and Pakistan* (1998)
Richard N. Haass and Morton H. Halperin, Co-Chairs; Cosponsored by the Brookings Institution

* †*Managing Change on the Korean Peninsula* (1998)
Morton I. Abramowitz and James T. Laney, Co-Chairs; Michael J. Green, Project Director

* †*Promoting U.S. Economic Relations with Africa* (1998)
Peggy Dulany and Frank Savage, Co-Chairs; Salih Booker, Project Manager

* †*Differentiated Containment: U.S. Policy Toward Iran and Iraq* (1997)
Zbigniew Brzezinski and Brent Scowcroft, Co-Chairs

†*Russia, Its Neighbors, and an Enlarging NATO* (1997)
Richard G. Lugar, Chair

* †*Financing America's Leadership: Protecting American Interests and Promoting American Values* (1997)
Mickey Edwards and Stephen J. Solarz, Co-Chairs

**Rethinking International Drug Control: New Directions for U.S. Policy* (1997)
Mathea Falco, Chair

†*A New U.S. Policy Toward India and Pakistan* (1997)
Richard N. Haass, Chairman; Gideon Rose, Project Director

Arms Control and the U.S.-Russian Relationship: Problems, Prospects, and Prescriptions (1996)
Robert D. Blackwill, Chairman and Author; Keith W. Dayton, Project Director

†*American National Interests and the United Nations* (1996)
George Soros, Chairman

†*Making Intelligence Smarter: The Future of U.S. Intelligence* (1996)
Maurice R. Greenberg, Chairman; Richard N. Haass, Project Director

†*Lessons of the Mexican Peso Crisis* (1996)
John C. Whitehead, Chairman; Marie-Josée Kravis, Project Director

†*Non-Lethal Technologies: Military Options and Implications* (1995)
Malcolm H. Wiener, Chairman

Managing the Taiwan Issue: Key Is Better U.S. Relations with China (1995)
Stephen Friedman, Chairman; Elizabeth Economy, Project Director

†*Should NATO Expand?* (1995)
Harold Brown, Chairman; Charles Kupchan, Project Director

---

*Available from Brookings Institution Press ($5.00 per copy). To order, call 1-800-275-1447.
†Available on the Council on Foreign Relations homepage at www. foreign relations. org.